A NEW VIEW OF TECHNOLOGY DEVELOPMENT AND ECONOMIC GROWTH

JOHN LOK

Contents

Preface

Introduction

    Our societies had been experiencing new technological development.Our business society had developed long time from farming period to manufacturing period, then to service industry period, till to nowadays technology service and manufacturing period. It bring this questions: Can technology or human behavior may influence economic development? How human behavior influences social change? How human behavior may help our future societies to bring economic growth? Can human behavior influence global economic growth? Can human behavior influences social change? Can smart phone invention bring economic growth? What does supply and demand economic society mean? Can technology bring positive consumer shopping emotion? Can non-manual driving public transport increase passengers number ? If it is true, which aspects of human behavior or how our behavior which will excite global societies to bring long term economic growth. I will attempt to indicate some human behavior may influence economic growth and explain why and how these human behaivoral factors may influence economic growth in behaivoral economic view.

Prologue

Table of content

Why has any individual country have many people invest share behavior which can influence the country's macro consumption desire?
Can technology influence human shopping behavioral change?
Why and how human behavior may influence the country's economic growth or recession?
Technology how impacts human behavior changing?
How and why employees behaviors may influence economy development?
Robots invention whether they can help organizations to raise efficiencies or inefficiencies?

Why social behavior may influence organizational strategy needs to be changed ?
Reasons why human behavior may influence economic recession or growth ?
How employee behavior influences organizational development?
Artificial intelligent Human clever and art creating ability methods
Why does technology raise online products sale demand and reduces shops products sale demand?
Does car technological development reach mature stage to help economic development?

Chapter 5 Technology how influences consumer demand changes
     Face reading technology and video camera recording
consumer behavior predictive differences
     ● Recommendation of face reading technology
is for confectionery food manufacturers and
ethnographic consumer behavior video
camera recording method to product

Constructive consumer choice process

● How constructive consumer choice process
measures which attribute factor(s) can influence
consumer chooses to buy any product or

Evaluating online sale methods

● Explaining what situation makes the
individual consumer doesn't accept
to use internet technology sale channel to
buy the product as well as it why
internet will cause negative purchase
emotion to any consumer to choose

to buy any manufacturer's products . p.113-120

REFERENCE
Chapter 6 Can non-manual driving public transport increase passengers number

What the psychological need differences between rail and bus and ferry passengers p.121-140
Reasons we need to improve public bus transport tool service quality
What rail passengers really want rail innovation improvement
What ferry passengers service improvement need
● How can ferry service be improved affordable, reliable, convenient, flexible and clean will get drivers out of their cars ad onto environmentally responsible to passenger ferries?
Future Human Transport Need Change p.141-161

How future our transport need change?
What factors influence our future transport need change?
How transport has changed from past to present?
Future Non-Manual driving vehicle How
Influences Public Transport Tool Passenger Need
Why and how non-manual driving car owners need raise public transport quality on travel time and fare aspects
How non human driving behavior can be influence by non-manual driving cars

CHAPTER ONE

Reason invention may bring economic growth

Can human behavior may help economic growth? Why human behavior and economic growth have close relationship? I believe that productivity growth in different industries, how the shares of

wages and profits, how taxation affects growth, how inventions which can bring global economic growth, create working chance, sale income chance, consumption chance, productivity chance,

wealth chance. These factors may bring global short term or long term economic growth. All of these factors hace close relationship between human invention and economic growth. I shall

explain as below:

For any kinds of things inventions example, are best regarded as a form of investments, and their volume depends in like manner, on their expected profitability. Investments opportunities

are recreated by inventions investment. However, inventions may not be economig growth factor, but there is a high profitability that prior circumstances will bring them about,

so learning from human past prior experience is important not just in scientific or engineering matters, but in other fields, such as business and social organization. So, research and development,

such as human invention behavior which has chance to bring long term or short term economic growth.

I mean that human invention may be one kind of investment opportunity to bring global economic growth in possibility, because human new knowledge learning behavior may attribute to global new business invention chance to bring unlimited economic growth chance in nowadays society.

Hence, human can not neglect to create ourselves " invention mind or invention behavior" in order to help global economic growth more easily. SO, human invention may be one kind helping

global economic growth new investment opportunuty, which is created from " human learning behavior". IN fact, an improvement in investmednt opportunity method may be created by human " any

kinds of new inventions behavior". SO, nowadays society, any kinds of new inventions of product, whcih ought help global societies to bring economic growth chance.

The theory of economic growth may be based on income, labor and land which every one kknows and which are adequate. However, nowadays society had changed, such as scientific invention example,

it can bring profit chance to business, creating job opportunities in global labor markets, such as smart phones, laptops, desktops, non-manual driving vehicles, electric energy cars invention

etc. any kinds of new scientific invention products, they can bring new scientifical products businessess chance, they must need to employ may manufacture labour, salespeople,

transport workers,logistic store workers, admin stafs, transport workers, product invention staffs , marketing promotion staffs etc. different job positions to let global human can have chance to find these jobs to do in order to earn income. Moreover, any kinds of scientific product inventions , which can bring many new jobs positions chance to let global unemployed people hace chance to work and earn incoime.Also, any kinds of new scientific products invention may create many new jobs chance to global and solve unequal wealth and income allocation problem to global human, even businesses have chance to sell these new scientific invention products to sell to global buyers to earn more profit.

I mean that " new products invention" may help global societies to reduce unemployment challenge and it can bring long term economic growth in global labour market view. Moreover, when any

kinds of new product inventions, such as battery energy vehicle, non-manual driving auto vehicle or public transport tools, home washing machines, televisions, radios, fans, smart phomnes,

laptops, electronic book reading tools, internet invention etc, different kinds of new scientific product inventions, they can bring " consumption opportunity" to let global consumers

have chance to buy any kinds of new scientific inventionw, which can also encourage global consumption rate raises in order to increase global wealth improvement rate speed rises up radidly.

So, global wealth rising rate whether which is rapid or slow, it depends on whether how many different kinds of new scientific products invention may be confirmed to scceed to sell in

global business market.

Hence, investment on invention, which may be tangible evidence to create economic growth in the distribution of income , wages and profits between global labor, scientific inventions of products sellers,and global scientific inventions of products consumers. They have close relationship to be influenced to increas economic growth speed whether they are rapid or slow from " global scientific new products inventions". If human product invention scientists can attempt to research how to invent any kinds of undiscovered new kinds of products inventions, for example, if global any kinds of scientific product invention scientistis can attempt to invest time to invent 100 kinds of new scientific products inventions in orde to provide global human have chance to buy to use. Then, these 100 different kinds of scientific invention products may help global new invention of scientific products sellers to provide many different kinds of new jobs vacancies to let global unemployed or job seekers have chance to work and earn income.

So, global unemployed rate will have chance to reduce in global societies. Moreover, they can also help these new scientific products sellers to bring " earning profit chance", even thes global " new product invention scientists who have earn product invention royalty income chance after they can invent any kinds of products in success.

Finally, global consumption market growth rate will bc influenced to rise up, when in the year, there are 100 new kinds of nre scientific products invention have been already sold to let global consumers hacew chance to choose the kind of target of scientific product to buy to use. So, global new economic growth rate speed , it can rise up rapid up or slow down, it depends on whether the year, global has how many kinds of new invention of scientific products" have been invented to prepare to sell in global scientific products sale market

in macro economic view.

Hence, economic growth and human invention behavior, which have cloase relationship . The list of anti-growth factors could be extended perhaps however. Hartwell (1983) has pointed out that economies have always contained a mixture of three main systems for making production, consumption, and distribution decisions namely, administered and market

free enterprise. It was the gradual freeing
of man's entrepreneurial talents from the bonds of custom and command
that finally resulted in the remarkable economic growth of the industrial
revolution. However, in the twrms of human history, sustained economic
growth is rare, and this suggests that several conditions (Needham's
Packet), rather than memely one or two , have had to be met before it earns
occur.

It is also the case, however, that its occurrence has at least in some
respects made its survival more probable. HUman scientific investment
has improved communications, such as smart phone, internet email and
increased education (learning) chance, such as distancel learning, AI
learning writing method, listening language learning method, reading e-
books from smart phone, laptop channel method, which can chance
traditional classroom leanring method to new scientific channel learning
method or which can change traditional telephone or post lewtter
communication method to nowadays sending email, smart phone calling,
whataps new scientific tool communication methos.

ON conclusion, the free societies are influenced by any kinds of new
scientific products inventions, Human had began to accept how attempted
to buy any kinds of new scientific products inventions to use. New scientific
inventions of products, which has bring more fashable of undiscovered new
scientifical inventions of products choice to satisfy human ourselves daily
new products invention using needs in our daily lives. SO, human scientists
whose any kinds of new products inventions which will bring more chance
to help global societies to create new social economic growth in global
societies.

Learning invisible hand economy theory
How may " inivisible hand " factor influence the smart phone manufacturer
products demand number increase?
The invisible hand is for the law of supply and demand explains how the
pull and push of these two factors serve to benefit sciety as a whole. In
simple, every consumer choose to buy the product, he/she pursues to earn
the most more interest to the manufacturer needs to produce the product
as its product may be of the greatest value to let the consumer intends only
his/her own gain, led by an invisible hand to promote the product to let the
consumer to make satisfaction to choose to buy the product.
In behavioral economic view, the invisible hand to the product

manufacturer may be " the consumer whose satisfactory feeling to use the product".So, the invisible hand meant that ir can not be touch , seen, it only brings feeling to let the consumer to feel. This feeling to the product is very mportant factor to excite the consumer to choose to buy the product, e.g. smart phone product the smart phone buyer's invisible hand factor may include: The smart phone can link to app to use internet service, download documents from smart phone , taking phonoes, watching movie, listening music, clock time etc. function, seeling different countries street locations, instead of general mobile talking function.

So, all of above factors will be future new smart phone main " invisible hand" factors to excite future smart phone buyers to make purchase decision to choose to buy the kind of smart phone among different kinds of smart phone products innovation , when they are manufactured to promote to smart phone market to sell.

So, in smart phone market supply and demand view, the smart phone manufacturer needs to innovate new smart phone products in order to let smart phone buyers fee its news phone buyers feel itsnew smart phone products have unique functions or features to excite its smart phone buyers to choose to buy its new kind of smart phone products, because smart phone buyers will be influences to make final smart phone purchase decision by invisible hand factors from smart phone different new function

.

Smart phone manufacturers need to innovate many new functions o future new kinds of smart phone manufacturing in order to bring new invisible hand satisfactory feeling to let any one smart phone buyer to feel whose new smart phone can bring the most unique satisfactory feeling to let them to feel. So, smart phone 's invisible hand factor is main influential factor to bring smart phone manufacturer's new smart phone demand number will increase or decrease. If the smart phone manufacturer can often innovate its smart phone products to let smart phone buyers feel more using satisfactory feeling to its new kind of smart phone more than its other similar kinds of smart phone manufacturers. Then, the smart phone manufacturer ought raise its smart phone purchase number demand easily.

What is smart phone opportunity cost?

Hence, the concept of opportunity cost factor means smart phone manufacturers need to forgone opportunities of time cost , design new kinds of smart phone products, e.g. smart phone pictures, colour and shape , future smart phone manufacturers need to concentrate more time to research how to innovate new featurers and function to let every potential smart phone buyers to bring more functions using satisfactory feeling in order to attract they choose to buy its smart phone product.

On conclusion, opportunity cost to smart phone manufacturers may be forgone spend more time on smart phone design, colour choice, shape choice aspects. Smart phone manufacturers need to spend more time on innovate new feature and function aspects in order to satisfy future smart phone using needs in global competitive smart phone smart.

Nowadays, our global economy seems to continue grow, but it also has possible to bring recession by any factors. This question concerns whether either human behavior can influence future global social economic growth or recession or technology can influence future global social economic growth or recession more? I shall attempt to indicate evidences to explain as below:

Firstly, on the one hand, when one country can manufacture new technological products, e.g. laptops, war weapons (non-manual driving flying war air planes, space rocket, smart phone etc. different

kinds of high technological products. For America example, US is one export high technogical products country. When its these different kinds of high development products manufacturers can sell to local and overseas customers. Then, they may earn high profit from both. Alsn US government can charge high profit tax from these high technologicalproducts manufacturers, when they can attract global many customers to buy their any kinds of high technological products. So, it seems that high technological products manufacturers may

help US government and US high technological products manufacturers to earn more US technological products sale income. Moreover, technology can help US country to grow up its economic development in long term, due to US manufacturers can concentrate on effort to invent any kinds of new technological products in order to persuade global buyers to chooce to buy their products in preference.

However, but on the other hand, I feel human behavior, such as talent high technological products inventors , they are the beginning main factor to help US to grow economy. The reason is because US which any kinds of high technological products must need talent human product scientists) themselves idea to invention. If themselves idea can influence global high technological products buyers feel needs to buy to use. Then, they must choose to buy US country's any kinds of these products in preference.

So, talent high technological product scientists will be US future economic growth source. If one high technological product scientists did wrong idea to the high technological

product manufacturers to manufacture the kind technological products. They can not influence global buyers feel needs to buy the kind of high technological product to use. Then, whose

idea of innovationm may not help US to develop itself eocnomy.

Hence, such as technological product case example, talent product scientists their idea innovation factor can bring more influential to US future economic growth easily. So, I conclude this criticism to explain why human behavior is more important factor to compare technology to influence the country's economy, because if the high technological product inventor whose dreams and iea to invent the kind of high technological product, if it can influence users feel useful feeling, e.g. smart phone product, it can attract phone users buy to use because it can use internet to gather global data, or read online news, read electonic books, listen music, watch movie, take photos, know the day weather, send and receive email, download document etx. different kinds of fuctions. SO, can let phone users feel smart phones can replace past traditional innovation of mobile phones and smart phones can influence global mobile users feel human ourselves can make phone calls in convenient in anywhere. Hence, smart phone product manufacturers can help themselves countries to earn high GDP income and increase high profit tax to give themselves governments. Otherwise, the traditional mobile phone products can not persuade phone buyers to choose to buy forever, because

they lack more functions to compare smart phones.

So, it explains why smart phone users personal using phone behavior is more important to influence the country's economy because when global every family begin to feel to use smart phones is themselve daily habit, they need smart phone to help them to do any matters, instead of general phone call at streets. So, their using smart phone behavior will influence they feel often need to change new mobdel of smart phone invention of product to replace old model of smart phone. Consequently, smart phone manufacturers need to continue to invent new and more functions of new model of smart phone products to satisfy future global smart phone users' need. Henvce, smart phone users' habitual using new model smart phone using behavior may bring global smart phone manufactuers long term manufacturing benefits in order to increase sale number chance. So, smart phone is one kind of high technological product may help any smart phone manufacturing countries to grow up economic growth easily. Also, smart phone inventor individual

idea and smart phone improvement skillful technology and smart phone user individual frequent chaning new model using behavior which may be main factors to

influence the country's smart phone sellers sale number. Such as, UK, US, Germany , CHina. Korea , they are global main smart phone manufacturers.

Economists call it " production -side growth" , which means that most companies, most of the time, made their (such as those countries smart phone manufacturers profit by cutting the cost of production). If these countries' smart phone manufacturers can cooperate to research how to improve more new functions of new model of smart phones to sellin global smart phone market. Consequently, it is possible that their production of smart phone cost may be influenced to reduce. Then, themselves future invention of new model

of smart phone product sale price may also be influenced to reduce, due to reducing production cost. Then, the global smart phone buyers number may be influenced to increase by reducing smart phone production cost. When these manufacturing smart phone countries, every year , their smart phone sale number Ccan increase to double time , even more.

I believe that smart phone technological product may help these countries to earn more profit tax, if these countries smart phone manufacturers need to research how to improve future smat phone functions to satisfy global future smart phone user individuia; " frequent changing new model of smart phone habitual satisfactory need". So, future smart phone technological product may be one kind of high technological product to help the smart phone manufacturing countries themselves economic growth.

Ecommerce may also help the country to grow economy. In the past, before twentieth century , this efficiency extends to the ways our economic goods spread around the country and the world. As the begining of the twentieth century , most markets , more local, most people bought things made nearby. But with the expansion system and then commercial air travel and the super-efficiency of containerized shipping, markets became national and eventually, global. Till to first century, since internet technological invention, it brings economic chance to let any countries local merchants may apply web-store internet platform to help them to sell

products to overseas buyers. They only need click to the overseas seller whose web store and then they canpay visa to buy the kind of product frm the online seller's web-store. So, many merchants , they own webstores to let overseas buyers can pay visa to buy the kind of product from themselves web-stores at their home countries conveniently. Then, the owning " more number of web-store sellers " countries government will have possible to earn high profit tax from these local webstore sellers. So, ecommercal sale internet technological platforms and global online buyers purchase behaviors , these two factors mau also influence the country's economy. If the country had many people like to buy any kinds of products from webstore, then they may influence the " owning more number of online sellers countries" their online seller profit increases, whether it is more or less sale number. Hence, whether e-commerce technology may help the country's government to grow GDP in technological product sale view. It depends on whether the country owns how many number of online sellers as well as how many online buyers number both for their products choice purchase chance. For example, when the country own high number people like to spend more time to stay at home to use internet. They do not like to walk on streets, they like to listen music and read books at homes more than going outside to do sports. Then, the country's people individual living habit will influence they choose to apply webstores to buy any things, if the country had
many people like to stay at homes more than leaving homes. SO, individual living behavior may also influence the country economy on online purchase view.

Finally, nowadays, some economists indicate that human ourselves behavior may be as full participants in Earth's cyclical processes of life and economy.
They think that human behavior, such as we are rational economic man, social adaptable humans, our daily behaviuors may bring direct or indirect influences
to global economy growth or recession. For share market example, before 21 century, share buyers need to go to banks or finance companies or share markets to buy the
company's shares. But, since 21 century, smart phone technological products had been invented. Nowadays global many share inventors began to choose to use smart phones
to buy and sell any companies shares in any time and any where

conveniently. So, smart phone invention had brought indirect influence to global share buyers'carrying on
sale and buying shares investing behavioral transactions in preferable choice. SO, smart phones and internet invention may influence global many share investors
shares investment behavior and investment attitude change. It seems that this both new technological invention can encourage future share investors accept to
apply smart phones to carry on shares buying and selling transactions more than visiting finance companies to enquire share agents their idea because, they can
apply smart phone to observe global any shares whether their prices will rise up or fall down immedicately. SO, smart phone and internet will changfe future share investors investment
behavior.

Two economic sociologists, DOnald Mackenzie and Yuval Miko, decided to reseach how share traders behaviors, however, by interviewing some of the share traders themselves. What did they discover? That the theory's increasing accuracy ovdr time was because the share traders had started to behave as if the theory ware true and so were using the model's predicted prices as a benchark for selling, their owning bids. FInancial economics, they
concluded " helped create in reality the kind of markets, it posited in theory. Ans as financial markets later learned, when those theories turn out to be flowed. If rational economic man can reshape our behavior in financial markets, he is vary likely to be reshaped our behavios in past. Hence, smart phone can influence future share buyers to do shares buying and selling decision in short time as well as it can persuade global share markets shares purchase number increases to bring economic growth.

CHAPTER TWO

Technology how influences cinema change

Nowadays, movie industry had been invented to apply online channel to let audiences to see any kinds of movies, even free ticket. In traditional, any kinds of movie must need audiences to buy tickets to enter cinemas to see movies. but, since internet invention, this kind of technology may let global audiences do not need to buy tickets to enter cinemas to see whose liking movies.

So, it brings this questions: Can online movie influence global cinemas reduce audiences number? Can online movie leisure industry be cinema movie leisure industry competitor? How cinema movie persuade online movie audiences to choose to buy tickets to enter cinemas to see movie in preference?

I feel that they are both substitute leisure product bewecn online movies and cinema movies. I mean that when one audience feels enjoy to enter cinema to see the kind of movie, who will forget to choose to see movie from online channel at homes. Although, online movies can let the movie audiences do not need to leave whose homes and they do not need to buy tickets to enter the cinema to see the kind of movie. However, cinema movie can let the audiences fee that they can sit down to see the movie and feel enjoying sound and see the movie from the large size warching screen in the cimena. Otherwise, when the audiences apply computer or mobiles to see the movie, they must not feel enjoyable to see the movie because any computers and mobiles whose watching screens are very small size, they must not let they feel more visable enjoyment to see the movies.

So, large size cinema watching movie screens and small size computer or mobile watching movie screens must be their main competitive strengths and weakness comparison. Although, the audiences may choose to rent movies to see from home televisions or choose not paying any to download movies to see from computers or mobile technological tools, when they apply internet to download the movie to see from computers or mobiles. But these audiences must feel more enjoyable to see visible images from cinemas whose large size watching screens, when they can sit down in the cinemas, even it is possible that global some cinemas had been beginning to auto-move the chairs to let their cinema audiences may feel exciting bodies moving feeling when they spend two hours to sit down on their chairs to see the movie in the cinema. S

So, auto-moving chairs feeling which may let many cinema audiences feel exciting to see any kinds of movies, due to they can enjoy exciting visable feeling and listening actual sound feeling, they can also feel their bodies are been moving from themselves auto-moving chairs in the cinema. So, cinema movies can let audiences feel this visable and listening and bodies moving feeling difference between online movies and cinema movies.

Consequently, future global cinemas may still apply their strengths , such as auto -moving chairs to audiences bodies feeling, large screen cinema watching screens visable feeling, actual listening sounds surround cinema inside sound environment feeling to let audiences feel visable and listening and bodies moving on chairs feeling to feel comfortable to see movies in cinemas. Hence, above these strengths will be any cinemas attracting audiences methods to compare seeing online movies channel.

CHAPTER THREE

Robot how influences labor behavioral change

Human Behavioral network job brings social economic benefits

What does human network job mean ? Why may human network job be popular? Why human network job behavior may influence economy ?

Nowadays internet is popular to use. We can apply internet to find data , search any new things, even earn money. Why does internet

may become huma network job source. For example, e-publish may be one kind of new human network job. Any authors may apply internet

channel to help them to sell electronic or paper books from e-publisher web store. They may apply facebook, you tub etc. any online

channel to promote themselves new books to let new readers to know whether when they may buy themselves favourable new topic books to read from electronic publisher web store.

Thus, future electronic publisher industry may help any authors to build internet network platform to help them to sell and promote

ot advertise their any one new electronic or paper book topic to let global any one reader to choose to buy their any new topic books from electronic publisher web store easily and conveniently. However, it implies that electronic network platform author may be one kind of future new human network job in our societies.

How electronic network platform author job may bring economy benefit in macro economy view? A person can have few friends, contacts and still be very influential if these few

friends and contacts are themselves highly influential, e.g. one author must not need to know any one reader in global society. When they like to choose any electronic books from electronic internet network platform. They may become the author's any one topic book buyer, when they feel the author's any one topic book is fun and attract they make decision to buth the strange author whose the topic book from electronic book publisher's platform web store conventiently in short time. Although, they are strangers, they do not know themselves , but the reader can understand what it way that made Google from writing platofrm to create new creative mind and typing network job method to replace traditional hand writing book method for global authors. It will be one kind of new human network writing job.

Hence, global any one reader can apply an innovative search engine , such as google.com to find whether whom author personal new topic books are value to read from internet.

Then, the electroniuc publisher's web store may be new book store platform sale network to help the author to sell many electronic or paper books from electronic network platform

in short time. So, internet may be future new network plaform to help global any one author to create network writing job absolutely. Furthermore, internet may be popular social media

to help any one author to build goold relationship between his/her readers. It is one kind of new network, human network job. New authors do not need to buy many paper books to prepare to put in any one book shop warehouse. Their every book can print on demand to reduce out of book stock in any one book shop. They may choose to sell either electronic books or paper books both from any one book publisher web store. So, electronic network platform may be one kind of good writing channel to help human authors to create income and it can also help authors to bring new creative mind and new topic fun content books to let readers to know and buy to read from electronic publisher network platform.

Why does human behavior may be one kind of new human network job to bring global economic advantages. ALthough, it may be free income or without inocme, but the person does the network behavior, his/her behavior may be bring advantages to influence many other people's health. For this case, when a worker in a coffee shop in an airport gets a vaccination againinst the flu, it does not only helps him or her stay healthy, but also helps the many travellers who might otherwise have been inflected if that workers caught the flu. So, the externality , the result implies the vaccination of even a part of a community conveys benefits to the whole community. For example, governments pay special attention to the vaccinations of school children, teachers, health mothers, and the elderly, categories of people particularly susceptible not only to catching, but also to transmitting a disease.

It is not accidential that governments are heavily involved with vaccination . When there are externalities, free market, fail to persuade individual incentives with society's

their the worker's decision of whether to get a vaccine ends up attracting whether other people get sick. The workers might not fully take all these other people's potential suffering into account when making her or his vaccination decision.

As Stanford University does many suggestions, understand this and tries to help them make the right decisions and so providers free flu vaccines for its staff and students.

Small pockets of unvaccinated individuals can allow a disease to gain a spread more widely well-being. For example, parent weighing the costs and benefits of a vaccine for their child is not always thinking of the consequences of that vaccination to other people. THese are markets in which subsidizing or regulating behavior can make everyone better off. Because the reason for requiring that a child be vaccinated before enrolling in school is not just to protect that child, because each child's vaccination affects others via potential contagions.

Robots take our jobs behavioral and economy influences

Robot job behavior brings economy influences

If one day robots can replace human to do simple, evcn complex jobs. They will bring what influences to our global societial economy.The popular economic refrain declares that the

global middle class is dying and robots will soon take our jobs, e.g. shopping center customer service jobs, library service jobs, cinema ticket sale jobs, restaurant kitchen cooker jobs,

even, bus drivers, taxi drivers etc. public transport driving jobs, accountant, doctors etc. professional jobs. Whether it is beautiful or petty matter if our future societies have many human jobs can be replaced to do from robots. Businessman must may reduce to employ employees and reduce to pay salary or wage, when robots can be replaced to do their employees tasks. But, societies must bring unemployement rate rises , due to societies will have many people loss jobs when their employers choose to buy robots to serve their clients or do any office tasks or customer service or cleaning etc.

tasks.

In micro economy view, employers may save money in long term, but in macro economy view, it will cause unemployment ratio rises , even crime rate rises when there are many people lose

jobs in societies. These models of doom, though, fail to account for the hundreds of businesses riding the waves of change in their industries when robots may be invented to replace human to do many simple , even complex tasks in our future societies.

WE may image that one small factory needs to manufacture fishes canes to sell to supermarket, the small , cheaper stuff and higher margin parts of the fishes manufacture industry. Before, this factory needs to employe many human factory workers need to help every fresh customer makeing the perfect fishing gear, designed for performance, durability, and cost in order to achieve to manufacture every fish cane in whole fished processing manufacturing stages. Every worker needs to spend about 15 to twenty minutes to finish every fish cane , till to delivery to any supermarket to sell. If this fish canes manufacturing factory can apply manufacturing robots to help them to finish any one working tasks , every robot can only spend five minutes to finish whole fresh fish cane manufacturing process. Thus, every robot can

help this factory save 10 to 15 minutes time to finsh every fish cane manufacturing process. IN fact, time is money, because when every robot can help this factory to reduce 10 to 15 minutes time to compare human worker. Then, this factory can finish about 20 fish canes in one hour if it can use robot to help it to manufacture fish canes. Otherwise, if this factory still use human workers to help it to manufacture fish canes, then it can finsh about 3 to 4 fish canes in one hour. SO, the manufacturing efficiency ensures that robots must help this fish manufacturing factory to raise fish canes number more than human workers. So, in robotic behavioral economy view, manufacturing robots must help this fish canes manufacturing factory to raise fish canes manufacturing number and deliver increasing number to supermarkets to prepare to sell every day. Robots can help this fish canes manufacturing factory bring manufacturing time saving, rising manufacturing efficiency, improving performance and reducing wages expenditure long time advantages in micro economy view. However, manufacturing robots can also bring disadvanages to society, e.g. increasing unemployment ratio, increasing crime rate,

this factory workers will lose jobs and income, they need earn social welfare from government and increasing government finance pressure in short time, even long time in macro economic view.

Stanford University graduate program in economics, Scott lecturer explained that "in demand and supply economic theory for robots supply and demand case, robots supply number increasing may influence human workers demand number decrease. It sometimes calls " the efficient frontier".

No specific human beings were mentioned in any of economics classes. As robots supply and demand in market case, They (robots) may be purely theoretical " agents" who reached to the most reasonable sale prices in order to persuade any one businessman buyer to make manufacturing robot buying decision whether robots can help him / her to bring how much saving time , saving money, saving cost, improving performance, efficiency economic benefit before he/she plans to reduce workers number when he/ she decides to apply robots to replace human workers in his/her factory or office or any service department, e.g. cinema ticket sale service, shopping center customer service, shopping center cleaning , supermarket customer service etc. service or sale tasks. When robots can replace human to do any one of these tasks in any organizations. So, robots may be human worker agents who reached to prices the way robots would react to a software command. There was nothing that explained why some people thrived and others did n't or why truly brilliant, hardworking people could fail when much lazier folks succeeded." Having been admitted to the Stanford University graduate program in economics, Scott lecturer hoped to get his answers there.

How robots influence our future social changing? Using the right technology can be a boon to your business in this economy. For internet example, it is easier than ever to find well-matched customers all around the world, to stay in contact with them, and to more quickly design the products they want. If you focus solely on being cutting -edge, though you risk letting the technology
take over what should be very robust relationships with your customers , employees, and colleagues. IN nowaddays society, technoligical advances and cutomation, personal
relationships in business are more crucial than ever. I mean that robots can not replace human to serve clients to let them to feel more comfortable and passion more easily. For shoe shop case example, if the shoe shop apply one robot to serve its clients to replace human shoe salesperson to serve

its shoe customers. Robots ensure that they can not persuade every shoe potential buyer to make shoe buying decision more easily when robots need to contact every shoe potential buyer. The reason is simple, because robots can not touch any one shoe buyer individual emotion very easier.

If the shoe buyer needs the robots to help him/her to choose any right shoe styles when he/she can not feel himself / herself can make the most right shoe style choice decision. The robots can not replace human shoe salesperson to make shoe style choice judgement more easily. They must need longer time to analyze whether which shoe style may be the most suitable to the shoe buyer. Otherwise, human shoe salesperson may attempt to make the most right shoe style choice decision to help any one shoe buyer to chooce the most right style shoe because he/she owns shoe style sale experience, shoe style knowledge, the most important reason is that they can feel every shoe customer individual emotion to touch whether he/she will feel comfortable or happy when they attempt to help every shoe customer to seek the most right shoe style in every shoe customer whole shoe searching processing. Othwerwise, serving robots are only one machine, they can not touch or feel every shoe customer individual emotion whether he/she feel comfortable or unhappy or happy when they need to contact them in whole shoe searching processing. Hence, I believe that some tasks robots can

not repalce human staff to do very easily. Otherwise, robots may bring disadvanatges to let any one businessman to loss his/her customers, due to robots can not touch every customer

emotion to compare human staff in service tasks more easily. Robots serving customer behaviors may cause money lose and customers number lose to the shop in micro economic view.

Intellectual human economic behaviors

What does intellectual human economic behaviors mean ? I believe that when we choose or decide to do intellectual behaviors, then our societies will be influenced to bring economic growth in consequence.I shall attempt to indicate pollution case to explain how and why eithet our intellectual or foolish behaviors may bring economic growth or recession in consequence as below:

On one hand, for air pollution social case aspect example, if we only consider to buy cars to drive for working aimr or holiday leisure aim. Then, our societies air will be polluted. Our health will be influenced to bad. Our car driving behaviors may cause global environment air pollution serously.

In long tiem, global air pollution will bring our bodies health to be bad. Although, ourselves car driving behaviors may bring our driving travelling leisure enjoyment and comfortable feeling in short time, also we so not need to pay public transport fare often, but we need to compensate ourselves health economic intangible loss due to air pollution , when cars number increases, dirty air will cause ouselves health to become bad.

In the result, we will need to pay more medical expenditure when we are old age, due to ourselves bodies will become bad, due to we breathe global dirty air every day, due to ourselves cars pollute air in long time, e.g. 10 to 20 years, even 30 more without limited air pollution environment. So, driving cars behavior may be one kind of human foolish behavior and our foolish behavior may bring ourselves future long time medical expenditure absolutely.

One the other hand, water pollution social aspect, if we often keep much rubblish to pollute sea, oil exploration porcessing pollute ocean , ships gas pollute ocaen, then fishes will eat polluted food and drive dirty water, due to global ocean is polluted.

In fact, because human only to conside how to buy boats to carry on leisure enjoyment activities, or catch cruises to travel on the sea. Also, oil manufacturers only consider researching anywhere to find new oil exploration places to manufacture oil product, when their oil exploration processes pollute ocarn . Consequently, global fishes drink polluted warer or eat polluted food. They will have poison. SO, human will have high chance to eat poison polluted fishes, due to fishes are poison or are polluted. So, human is doing foolish activities, we only hope to find oil exploration places to pollute ocean or we only spend money to buy ticket to catch ships to travel anywhere in global ocean. All of these human foolish behaviors will bring pollution to global ocean. On consequently, we will need to compensate to eat polluted or dirty or poision fishes, ourselves bodies health will be bad. In long time, we need have high chance to pay medical expenditure when we are old. So, pollution case may be one good example to explain how and why human foolish behavior may influence ourselves future need to compensate serious medical loss.

All of these human foolish behavior will bring pollution to global ocean. On consequently, we will need to compensate to eat polluted or dirty or poison fished , ourselves bodies health will be bad. In long time, we will have high chance to pay medical expenditure, when we are old. So, pollution case may be one good example to explain how and why human ourselves intellectual or foolish behaviors may influence future long time economic loss or economic growth or recession in micro and micro economic view.

On another water pollution aspect hand, if we often keep rubbish to sea, oil exploration processing pollutes ocean and ships' gas pollute ocean, then fishes will eat polluted food and drink dirty water, due to fishes will eat polluted food and drink dirty sea water because the global ocean is polluted seriously.

In fact, because human only consider how to buy boats to carry on any leisure water activities, or catches cruises to travel on the sea. Also, oil manufacturers only consider any where to find oil exploratin places to manufacture oil products from ocean, when their pol exploration processes can plooute ocean. Consequently, global fishes drink polluted water or eat direty food. They will have poison. So, human will have high chance to eat poison fishes.

Otherwise, such as pollutin case, it can infuence inflation or deflation. Consequently, the reason indicates supply and demand theory. If air pollution is serious, then we will consider health issue, global cars demand number may be influenced to reduce, when global cars number demand will reduce, global car prices and supply number will need to change to fall down in order to attract or persuade global car consumers choose to make car purchase decision.

Hence, global car manufacture number and car price will be influenced to reduce, due to global air pollution issue. Consequently, deflation will occur because when the country citizen usually does not spend much extra saving money to buy car expensive goods. Money value will be low. Otherwise, if global cair pollution is not serious, human considers to buy cars to enjoy driving leisure lives. So, global car demand is influenced to increase , also global car price will also influenced to increase.

Consequently, gobal human will choose to buy cars to drive. Due to we accept to spend extra saving to buy expensive car goods. Car sale price and supply may be influenced to rise up. Money value is influenced to reduce. Inflation may be influenced, due to global car consumers number increases, we would not have extra money to spend easily. Car expensive goods expenditure influences our spending habit to avoid to make car purchase decision more easily. So, human intellectual or foolish activities may bring inflation or deflation consequency in possible indirectly in macro economic view.

On conclusion, above pollution case explain that how and why human intellectual or foolish economic behaviors may bring inflation or deflation consequency as wll as economic growth or recession consequency as well as any goods demand and supply increasing or decreasing consequency. It implies that human behavior may have indirect relationship to influence any goods demand and supply number to either increase or decrease result as well as any goods price will be influenced to increase or decrease in micro and macro economic view.

The relationship between social change and human behavior

Why does economic changes may influence human individual behavioral change? I shall attempt to indicate shopping behavior and staying at home behavior to explain their case and effect relationsip as below:

Human behavior can be influenced by economic change or economic change can be influenced by human behavior? Why does recession may influence consumers reduce shopping desire? In social recession suitation, it is possible that many people lose jobs suddenly, due to businessmen lose many customers. They need to make decision to reduce employees number in order to continue to keep businesses. Consequently, many firms (organizations) their employees may lose jobs. When they have much time, due to lose jobs, they will feel to avoid to spend too much time and money to go to shopping often. Many losing jobs people, they will often stay at homes. So, they will reduce time to go to shopping, then non essential products won't their preferable choice purchase products. Hence, recession will change many losing jobs people their shopping or consumption desires to avoid to buy non essential products often . Usually when economic boom, many people have jobs to do because consumers number must increase when many people have jobs to do. Then, many people can accept to spend money to buy non essential products often. Many people feel spend time to go to shopping can satisfy their purchase of any kinds of new products useful psychology or desire. So, recession is one good example to explain it can influence many people do not like often to leave homes to go to shopping easily. Many people like to stay at homes, becaue they feel worry about spending too much shopping time when they leave homes. Their staying home time is one good negative shopping behavior example. So, economic change may influence human individual behavior changes , they have direct cause and efect relationship in behavioral economic view.

May human behavior influence economic change? Is it possible that human behavior may bring the country social economic change in macro economic or micro behavioral economic view ? I shall indicate publishing industry example. Do you feel that if there are many students feel learning is very important when they read many books or many of students feel interesting to read or they have reading new books in habit, then it is possible that the country will have many students like to spend time to go to any book shops to choose the books, they feel that they can help they learn new knowledge. Then the country will increase students number, they often spend time to visit any one book shop every week. Their visiting book shops behavior which may become their habits. So, the country will increase students number, they often spend time to visit book shops. Also, it implies that visiting book shops behaviors may be their behavioral habits.

So, when the country has many students often spend time to visit book shops , their visiting book shops behaviors may help any one book shop to raise books sale chance. So, the country's student individual often visiting book shop behaviors, their habitual visiting book shops behaviors must may assist help any one book shop to increase books sale number absolutely.

Consequently, any one book shop , its books sale bumber must be influenced to increase to increase because the country will have many students like or feel need visit book shops habit in order to choose any suitable books to buy to read at home in order to raise themselves learning effort. When the country has many bok shops often have many students visit their book shops, then their books sale number may be influenced to increase. It explain why student individual visiting book shop behavior may help any one book shop sale number increases also.

How human productive behavior may influence economic development

May any country which citizen behavior assist themselves country development? It is one cause and effect economic question. I mean that if the country itself citicen can not concentrate mind or energy to choose to do one kind of industry in order to let themselves country can bring the most benefit, then whether the counry itself economy can bring the most serious economic benefit. I shall attempt to indicate these countries themselves indistry choice to explain whether these countries themselves citizen productive behavior may help themselves countries to achieve the largest economic benefits. I shall indicate as below:

New Zealand farmer individual wine productive behavior

For New Zealand country example, this country concerns itself effort is foucs on farming agricultural aspect. So, this country has many farmers concentrate on farming agricultural aspect. May New Zealanders choose to spend time to produce different kinds of wines, e.g. wine or red grape wine is for the people are eating meat, or they are eating dinner.

When these New Zealanders their behaviors choose to do farming or agriculture to grow and produce different kinds of taste of white or red grape wine drinking products job. Themselves grape agriculture behavior will influence these New Zealanders themselves, they can learn how to improve different kinds of grape wine drinking products in order to achieve every kinds of white or read grape wines taste improving aim during their white or red grape producing process.

Why can New Zealander every individual white or read grape wine producers improve their white or read grape wine taste more easily? In behavioral economic view, it can explain that why any one New Zealander white or read grape wine producer can be encouraged or excited or persuaded to concentrate nervous and energy and effort to learn how to improve their white or red grape wine products easily.

In fact, New Zealand is one agricultural food export country. It has good natural environment resource , e.g. land, seed to provide any one farmer to produce themselves any kinds of agricultrual food products, e.g. fruit, or wine food products. Because New Zealanders know themselves country has enough natural resource . So, in common, many New Zealanders choose to attempt to do farming agricultural jobs in order to export themselves any kinds of fruit or meat or wine products to overseas or sell to domestic in order to earn profit.

So, when these New Zealand farmers number has been increasing every year. This country farmers will feel themsleves competition between this New Zealand farmers themselves are serious due to they may feel New Zealanders choose to do agriculture businesses in order to export themselves different kinds of farming food to overseas or sell to local to earn profit.

Hence, when many New Zealand farmers feel that farmers number has been increasing every year. They will feel themselves competition is serious. They must need to spend much time and nervous and effort to research what method is the best how to produce the best taste of white or red grape wine products in order to let local or overseas wine buyers to choose to buy his/her producing white or read grpae products to drink.

Hence, in competition psychological view, may influence many New Zealand white or reaad wine producers had been beginning to change their learning behavior on researching what method is the best in order to produce the best quality of taste red or white wine products to sell in order to attract overseas or local white or read grape wine drinkers to choose to buy his/her wine products. Their behavior will focus on learning how to raising or improving white or read grape wine taste method more than only focus on producing a large number white or red grape wine products. They believe wine quality is more important to compare wine producing number. So, New Zealand wine producers themselves wine producers behaviors have been changing on concentrating on researching wine quality method aspect more then wine producing number aspect in behavioral economic view.

America high technological productive behavior

For America example, US is one high technological country, it owns many high technological knowledge talent inventors, e.g. computer science inventors. Hence, US must attract many diferent countries owning high technological computer inventors choose to go to US to develop their computer science profession career. Also, it seems that when many computer science inventors or professions choose to go to US to develop themselves computer science new career. In behavioral economic view, due to their leaving themselves countries choice, which may bring influence themselve country job behaviors need to be changed. They must need to adapt US new live. Because they will forgive their past computer science job. These computer science professionals need to spend time to adapt US new lives. They " past computer science job behaviors" will need to be changed to their new US any computer employer's new computer science job model.

Because their traditional computer science jobs needed to be forgot in their themselves countries. They will feel their old computer science job knowledge and behavior needed to change in order to let their US any one new of computer company employer feels satisfactory to accept their new working behavior in any one US computer organization.

So, on the other hand, many US computer company employer will feel that they must need time to accept any one new overseas computer science professions their working behaviors, their working attitude daily, because these foreign comouter science professional, their past computer working behaviors and working attitude must be different to US domestic computer science professions.

In behavioral economic view, these overseas computer science professions, their working behaviors and attitude must be needed to change in order to adapt any one US new computer company itself domestic or local computer science professional stafs themselves daily working behaviors and attitude because these overseas and local computer science professionals must need to team work together.

In behavioral economic view, it is only one way that foreign computer science professionals must need to change themselves past country traditiona daily working behaviors and attitude in order to cooperate with these US local computer science professionals in teams more easily.

Consequently, if these foreign compute science professionals can change their past working behaviors and attitude to let any one US local computer science professional feels to cooperate with them easily in short time. Then, the US computer company itself whole computer professional teams themselves efficiencies will be influenced to raised or improved by the changing past working attitude and working behaviors of these foreign computer science professionals. So, in behavioral economic view, only if US any one computer company hopes itself computer teams themselves efficiency can be raised or improved when it decides to employ foreign computer science professionals and US domestic computer science professionals. They need to work in teams together. They must need to let these foreign computer science professionals to know how to change their working behaviors and attitude to let their domestic computer science professionals feel easy to work together. Then, the US computer company itself whole team efficiency must be rasied or improved easily in short time.

● China share market investing behavior

For China share market example, economic development depends on financial market. Because if many Chinese have interest to invest to carry on shares buying and selling activities in orde to learn how to earn shares interest and share profit when the China shareholder can make decision to sell himself/herself shares in the the high price, then he/she can earn money when he/she can sell the China company's shares in the high sale share price position.

If China has many Chinese like to spend time to carry on investing shares activities. Themselves shares buying and selling behaviors will influence China has many companies can increase fund from many Chinese shareholders in order to have enough money to expand or develop themselves businesses in China in long term.

Consequently, when China can have many Chinese like to attempt to carry on buying and selling shares investing behaviors in China share market. Themselves buying and selling shares behaviors can help many Chinese companies have effort to increase enough money or capital in order to continue to do their businesses in long term absolutely. So, it explains why when many Chinese become shareholders , they can assist China will have many companies continue to develop their businesses if many Chinese like to carry on shares buying and selling investing behaviors in long time in China financial investment market nowadays in behavioral economic view.

Why has any individual country have many people invest share behavior which can influence the country's macro consumption desire?

I shall apply shares market buying and selling investment behavior to explaiin why shares investment behavior which may impact the country's overal consumption desire as below:

In behavioral economic view, I assume that when the coutry has many people have interest to attempt to carry on shares buying and selling investment behavior, then their frequent shares buying and selling behaviors which may bring negactive consumption desire or shopping desire of these shares investors their consumer behavior.

The reason is simple, when the country has many share buyers number suddenly been increasing rapidly. Consequently, these large group share investors must need to spend much time to research any kinds of company shares variations, whether when their share prices will rise up of fall down in order to achieve buying the company's shares in the lowest price and selling the company's shares in the highest price level in order to earn profit.

Basic on this reason, they must need to spend much extra time to research share prices changing behavior every day, e.g. one working person will wait to leave his/her job, after he/she can spend time to gather data to research the day's share price changing behavior after dinner. So, the working person's right time may be his/her share price market research behavior. Before he/she may spend his/her night time to go to shopping after dinner, but nowadays, he/she will fogive to do his/her shopping behavior before dinner or after dinner at hight sometime. He/she will make decision to spend much night time to turn on computer to click on share market website to research his/her share purchase choice to investigate whether his/her share price whether it rises up or falls down at the moment in order to make his/her share buying or selling decision at ever night time.

I mean the when the country has many people are share investors, their shares investment behavioral spenging time which will influence many shops lose customers at might often because the country will have many people feel need to spend night time to turn on computer or watch television to investigate share price variation. So, the country will have many people / share investors choose to stay at home in order to carry on share price variation investigation behavior, they need to listen share market update news from radios or watch the share market update news from computer or TV at home every night. Consequenly, they must reduce times to leave themselves homes at night. So, their shopping behavior also will be reduced. Because these share investors feel need to spend time to investigate share price variation news at homes which can bring economic benefits (high opportunity benefits) when they choose to forgive to leave homes to go to shopping times (opportunity cost) every night.

On conclusion, it seems that when the country has many people are share investors, then their share price investigating behavior may bring negative shopping emotion at night. Consequently, the country's any one shop may lose many customers from this share investor consumer group in behavioral economic view. Hence, when the country's share investors number had been increasing rapidly, it will influence any shops lose many customers from this share investing customer group at night frequenly in short time, even long time in behavioral economic view, because their shopping desires or shopping emotion will be brought negative feeling when they make decisions to spend much time to listen radios or watch TV or computers share price update nes at night. Hence, share market will bring negative impact to influence consumer shopping desire or negative shopping emotion in behavioral economic view.

Can technology influence human shopping behavioral change?
Nowadays, technological development has reached mature stage, whether technological mature stage may bring positive or negative shopping emotion influence to global consumers. I shall aplly internet inventin or ecommerce shopping channel tool to explain whether internet technology can bring postive or negative influence to global consumer behavior in behavioral economic view.

Internet is a good technological tool, it brings e-commerce business chance. In fact, commonly, global has have many businessmen choose to use internet channel to carry on their products transactions between global online-buyers and their electronic websites. So, global many shoppers had begun to feel online shopping is more convenient to compare visiting shops shopping. Their shopping behaviors have been changed from internet technological tool. Global has many shoppers choose to buy any products from any overseas or local businessmen their web stores. They only need to spend time to find any businessmen their webstores to choose the most suitable products to pay visa to buy from their webstores. at homes. So, in general, global had have may shoppers had changed their shopping behaviors from visiting shops to visiting webstores at homes often.

So, it seems that internet technological tool had influenced global many shops disappear, but internet webstores will be replaced their actual shops on streets. Some of businessmen either they choose webstores to replace shops or choose websotes and shops both or still keep shops only. Hence, internet tool influences global businessmen have three kinds of products sale channels to let globa local and overseas consumers to choose how to buy their products.

However, in fact, many of global shoppers, youngers and olders had begun to accept to buy any products from webstores. They feel to spend time to leave homes to visit shops , their shopping behaviors will be wasted time to not essential part to their daily lives. Hence, since internet technological invention, it had changed many consumers their traditional visiting shops shopping habit to change to buying products from webstores channel.

However, on the one hand, internet creates webstores ecommerce shopping channel to let global many consumers do not need to leave homes to go to shopping. It brings negative visiting shops shopping emotion to global general consumers nowadays. But on the other hand, it also brings positive visiting internet webstores shopping emotion to global general consumer nowadays. So, it seems that global many consumers feel that they often do not need to spend much time to go out shopping. Many global consumers feel convenient and enjoy to choose any products to buy from different internet webstores, when the online buyer chooses the most suitable product, he she only needs to pay visa card to buy the product from the online seller's webstore conveniently at home.

Hence, online shopping can bring economic benefit to online buyers, e.g. avoiding walking time or spending transport fare to visit the shop to go to shopping, shortening or reducing shopping time to do another important matter.

On conclusion, global many consumers began feel online shopping can bring more economic benefits on shortening shopping time, avoiding transport fare spending aspect. So, online shopping will be popular shopping behavior for future long time. It may encourage global many shoppers can make rapid shopping decision in short time in order to carry on any products buying transaction to global any one online shopper in short time easily in behavioral economic view. So, global many businessmen had begun to build themselves one attraction webstore in order to persuade different countries consumers to choose to click themselves webstores from internet channel to buy any kinds of products in short time easily.

So, internet technology had changed consumers traditional shopping behaviors to build positive online shopping emotion as well as raise online sellers' any products sale chance easily in behavioral economic view.

Why and how human behavior may influence the country's economic growth or recession?

When one country has many people choose to do the same matter for one period, whether their behavior may influence the country's pvera; economic growth or recession . I shall attempt to indicate cases toexplain their relationship as below:

For flowing rubblish behavioral case example, do you feel that when the country has many people often flow rubblish on the streets, instead of their flowing rubblish behavior may bring streets dirty? But, their flowing rubblish behavior may explain that this country has people may have enough money to buy food to ear, or enough cloths to wear, enough bottles of water to drink, even they may have enough money to buy new television, radio, refrigeraters , washing machines, desktops or laptops electronic home products from old to new to use in order to satisfy their living needs. So, when they flow old electronic home products, their flowing old home electronic products behaviors may seem that they have cnough money to buy other new home electronic products to replace old home electronic products to use at homes.

However, it seems thaat this country ought have many people have jobs to do. So, many of them, they can easy to make purchase decison to flow any old home electronic products and buy any new home electronic products to use . Because this country has many people have jobs to do. So, they can often not use old home electonic products to become rubblishs to flow on streets after they had bought any kinds of new home electronic homes.

In fact, it also implies that this country's economy grows rapidly. So, many businesses can glow up rapdly. When they expanded their businesses, they must need to increase employees number in order to let they help themselves to raise productivity or serve their clients absolutely. So, when the country has many businesses can grow up, it seems that its economy must be better or it is improved to compare past. Due to many different kinds of home electronic products had been often bought to use by this country people in this period. So, this country's any streets can be observed that expensive electronic home products were flowed on streets anywhere. then, this country will have many electronic home products sellers can sell their home electronic products very easily. When this country has many people can find any kinds of jobs to do easily. So, due to unemploymen rate had been decreasing.

In behavioral economic view, as this many electronic home products rubblish country case, we can observe this country may have many people have jobs to do. So, consumption number has been increased long time. So, cheap food, or expensive home electronic products may be rubblish on any streets. This country's people , their flowing rubblish behaviors may be explained that many of people have enough jobs to do, so they have ability to buy any good taste food to eat or buy any kinds of expensive electronic home products to use. So, this country's economy may be improved for this long period. So, in behavioral economic view, when this country can have many electronic home products rubblishs are flowed on anywherer in streets frequently. It seems that this country will have many people have jobs to do, so it causes they often change old home electronic products or replaced them easily, when they have enough income to spend to buy any kinds of new home electronic products to use at homes easily. Moreover, their flowing old electronic home products behaviors also indicate that this country has many people their salaries may be increased in possible from their emplyers. When this country can have many different kinds of home electornic products are sold. It means that this country's electronic home products needs or demand had been increasing, due to many people have jobs to do and income increases to excite their living of needs also improve. Consequently, this country may seem have better economic improvement. We can observe from this country's electronic home products rubblish increasing income in theis period.

On conclusion, this country ought experience economic growth at this period. So, " flowing expensive electronic home rubblish increasing number " may seem that this country's economic growth is rapidly in this period, due to many people have jobs to do as well as salaries increase in this period.

Technology how impacts human behavior changing?

Technology how influences human behavior to bring changing? For example, online share purchase and sale transaction from smart phone brings share investor can do share buying or selling transation in any where and any time conveniently, non manual driving auto vehicle, bring car owner feels comfortable and spends free time to do other matter, e.g. reading, listening mucis in himself or herself car freely. electrical energy vehicle can help car owner to reduce air polluton and it can brings the drivers do not feel drive long time in any journeys in order to avoid air pollution for environmental protection responsible car drivers in our societies. Thus, they will drive long time in any journeys when they can drive electronic energy cars to replace oil energy cars.

However, online technology can also bring consumers can choose to stay at homes to buy any things from seller individual online webstore conveniently. Such as online technology can bring shoppers do not need to spend much time to visit shops to buy any things. They can choose any kinds of products from any online sellers individual online webstores conveniently at homes. Online technology excite busy consumers can make purchase decision easily as well as it can help online sellers sell any kinds of products from internet easily.

In behavioral economic view, technology can change human behavior to be improved, it can let human feels comfortable, more free time ro use, rapid making any decisions, such as apply smart phones to make share purchase or sale transaction decision, online shopping decision, even travelling any where decision in short time, when the traveller finds the most cheap hotel accommodation room price and air ticket price frm any travel agent online tourism webstore, then the potential travel customer can follow the online hotel accommodation price and air ticket price data to make decision when to buy the air ticket from the airline travel agent or make decision when to prebook which hotel accommodation room to go to the country to travel from online travel agent tourism webstores. So, technology can encourage global any country travelers to make anywhere to trvel rapidly. If the traveler can find the country's general hotel rooms and airline tickets prices had been decreasing more sightly. The traveler may make travel decision to choose the country to travel in short time, then he/she can prebook the country;s any hotel room and airline ticket to pay by visa fraom the country's any hotel and airline travel agent webstores., before one week, even one month or more easily. Hence, online technology can also encourage traveler individual frequent travel times to be increased, due to global travelers can find any hotel rooms and airline tickets prices from internet conveniently at homes. They do not need to spend time to visit any airline travel agent to enquire travel choice country's hotel rooms prices and airline ticket prices. They can compare global travel of countries choices ' all hotels rooms and airline agents air tickets prices to make prebook airline seat and hotel room decision before one week, one month even six months early.

On conclusion, online technology can encourage global travelers can make travelling any where and when traveling time desicions easily. It can excite tourism industry develops in long time. Also, such as electricity cars invention can encourage environment protection car owners do car purchase decision easily, because they can choose to drive electronic energy cars to replace oil energy cars in order to avoid air pollution occurs easily. So, electronic cars can increase electronic car purchasrs number, due to many of environmental protection attitude of car owners can choose to drive electricity cars to bring air cleans, even non -manual driving cars can encourage lazy driving and free time driving car owners to choose to buy non-manual (artificial intelligent) cars to drive , because they can spend much free time to read, listen music or do any matters in themselves cars, they do not need to drive cars, robotic (AI) auto driving machine is such one non-manual driver to help them to drive themselves cars confidently. So, non-manual driving cars can attract lazy and enjoying free time driving car owners to choose to buy to replace traditional manual cars to drive easily. Moreover, online share transaction can help any share investors to make share buying and selling decision in short time easily. When they can apply smart phones technological tool to carry on share buying and selling activities easily. They can observe any share rising or falling price suitation from smart phones in any where any any time easily. So, smart phone technology can help global any shareholders to make share purchase and sale transaction easily. So, technology can encourage human makes decision in short time rapidly.

How and why employees behaviors may influence economy development?

In behavioral economy view,I believe the country's any organizational employees behavior may bring indirect relationship to influence the country's long term economic development. I shall indicate past manufacture industry social development period to explain their relationship. For many countries' past business activities had belonged to manufacturing industry, such as US, UK past before 1980 year, it focused on steel manufacturing and steel manufacturing related machine products. So, US, Uk developed countries manufacturing industries may be past main country's economic income sources. I assume US , UK past had one million number different kinds of industries. They ought had about seven houndred thousand number organizational businesses were belonged to manufactured industry. They may include:

Steel manufacturing and steel related machine manufacturing, e.g. vehicle manufacturing, home appliances, e.g. washing machine, television, radio, refrigerate cooler, heater, air condition etc. different kinds of different kinds of steel -related manufacturing machine, they were manufactured from US, UK steel machine manufacturers. So, US, Uk the other three hundred thousand number industry may be general service industry, e.g. hotel service, restaurent, cinema, public transport service, tourism lesiure , wine bar, supermarket etc. different kinds of non-manufacturing industries business organizations were operated in UK, US past before 1980 year.

So, in UK, US developed countries industry development history, they ought have high percentage of businesses belonged to steel related manufacturing machine and steel products. Also, in the past before 1980 year, US, Uk business employers , they employed many workers are manufacturing workers. They needed to spend long time to work in factories. They were skillful workers, and they are trained to manufacturing cars, washing machine, television, heater, etc. even steel itself different kinds of steel related products to prepare to deliver to their shops to sell to US, Uk local or overseas clients.

So, I believe that past UK, US ought employ many employees, they belonged to skillful manufacturing workers, manufacture increasing steel machine or steel related machine number of products rapidly daily. So, if UK, US had had many of these manufacturing factories owned high skillful workers, then their manufacturing steel-related machine or steel both kinds of products number must be influenced to raise rapidly. Consequently, their steel machine manufacturing products would been exported to overseas or would been sold to local both markets , they may be influenced to raise sale number. They (these manufacturing workers) needed to be trained to know how to manufactur these different kinds of machine products in the efficient teams and they ought to be trained to raise their efficiencies in order to shorten time to manufacturing many kinds of steel related manufacturing machine or steel itself products rapidly. So , if their efficiencies and manufacturing performance was improved, these US, UK any one manufacturing worker and their teams ought achieve raising productivities significantly.

Hence, when past UK, US manufacturing industry development period, if these two countries' any manufacturing factories could have many manufacturing workers could be trained to be skillful and proficient manufacturing workers. Then, in past every day to these factories workers, they ought help their steel or steel related manufacturing employers to raise any kinds of machine or steel products number in every team. So, when past in the manufacturing industry development, US, UK could have many factories' manufacturing workers themselves steel or steel related machine products manufacturing skill could be trained to to improve to any kinds of these machine or steel manufacuring products quality as well as their products number could be influenced to raise by themselves skillful improvement significantly every day.

Then, what would be influenced to occur to past UK, US manufacturing industry period? In behavioral economic view, when these two manufacturing industry developed countries, such as UK, US , if they had many factories workers can be trained to improve their skill in order to achieve any kinds of steel or steel-related machine products quality could be improved as well as products manufacturing number could be also increased absolutely.

In consequence, past UK and US both countries ought increase themselves any kinds of steel and steel related machine products number to be supplied to themselves local shops to let local clients to choose any one kind of machine manufacturing products to buy easily as well as they could also export to supply overseas any countries to buy their different kinds of steel or steel related machine products to let overseas steel or steel related manufacturing machine product buyers, they can have many of these different kinds of these steel or steel-related different kinds of manufacturing machine from UK and UK these both countries easily to compare other countries.

On conclusion, I believe that past US, and UK macro manufacturing industry income GDP would increase significantly. So, they would have good economic growth performance because when many of these manufacturing workers themselves manufacturing effort could be improved. So, it explained when employees manufacturing abilities can influence economic growth indirectly.

Robots invention whether they can help organizations to raise efficiencies or inefficiencies?

In behavioral economic view, in any organizations, when the organization hopes its worker teams can raise efficiencies , the organization may choose to increase more workers number and/or it can provide training to improve these workets themselves skills in order to raise their efficiencies. For one warehouse example, when the warehouse increases many goods , they are needed to delivered these goods from the shelves to the delivering destination locations. If this warehouse supervisors feel these workers themselves goods delivery speeds are slow, which is possible due to this warehouse's workers number is not enough. So, this warehouse supervisor ought increase workers number in order to increase their goods delivery speed in order to deliver goods from the shelves to every indicated goods delivery destination in order to let any one lorry driver can transport the right kinds of goods and ensure the accurate goods number to transport to any one client home rapidly.

However, if this warehouse supervisor planed to buy several warehouse goods delivery robots to assist these warehouse workers to find the right kinds of goods from shelves and then deliver to the right destination location in the warehouse. So, these warehouse orkers can concentrate on counting the accurate goods number and ensuring the right kinds of goods in order to prepare to let lorry drivers to transport these goods to these goods of buyers themselvers homes rapidly. Consequently, in the first step, robots can concentrate on finding th right goods from shelves and delivers them to the right goods transportation of location destination. Then, in the second step, these warehouse workers can concentrate on counting the accurate goods number and ensuring the right kinds of goods in order to prepare to put them to the lorry. Consequently, when warehouse robots and warehouse workers can cooperate to work together, the most important, robots, can deal on finding the right kinds of goods and deal on delivering the accurate number of goods of job duty as well as these warehouse workers can only concentrte on counting the right kinds of goods number in order to avoid it has none any mistake of wrong kinds of goods and inaccurate goods of delivery number to be transported to the lorry and to deliver to any one buyer's home.

So, it seems that warehouse robots ought help any one warehouse worker to raise himself efficiency and avoid goods delivery of mistake occurrence easily as well as their help to warehouse workers that can let any one goods buyer feels their goods can be delivered to their homes rapidly. Moreover, warehouse robots can also help these warehouse workers to raise efficiencies because warehouse robots can help them to shorten goods delivery time between any one shelf and any one goods delivery destination of location in the warehuse because robots may help them to find the right kinds of goods from the right shelf in the short time. So, any one worker does not need to spend long time to seek anywhere is the right shelf location for the kind of goods when the kind of goods are needed to deliver to the buyer's home from lorry. Warehouse robots can help them to do this aspect of " finding the goods from the right shelf in short time job duty". So, any one warehouse worker only needed tospend less time to do the counting of any right kind of goods number and ensuring the right kind of goods job duty. Consequently, this warehouse 's any one worker, his any one kind of goods delivery time may be reduced, because robots' assistance and they may have more confidence to avoid mistake to deliver the wrong number of goods and/or the wrong kind of goods to any one goods buyer's home.

On conclusion, it seems that warehouse robots ought may help any one warehouse worker to raise efficiency for any one team in the warehouse as well as the warehouse any one supervisor does not need to spend much time to observe any one worker individual performance for " goods delivery job duty aspect" because their goods delivery job duty that had been replaced to do by these several warehouse robots. Robots can achieve the more accurate of right kinds of goods and the right number of goods delviery job performance to compare any one of human warehouse worker themselves right kinds of goods of delivery and right number of goods of delivery job performance. So, when robots can participate to cooperate with this warehouse's any one worker to do their goods of delivery job duty in this warehouse every day. Then, robots can raies any one of supervisor individual confidence in order to let they do not need to spend time to observe any one of worker individual whose goods of delivery job performane. They can concentrate on supervising any one worker whose goods transport to lorry in the final step in order to avoid to deliver wrong goods number and / or wrong kind of goods to any one goods buyer's home every day. Consequently, this warehouse's overall teams of their delviery of goods performance many be improved by robotss' participatin to goods of delivery task as well as this warehouse's oveall teams themselves efficiencies may be influenced to raise by robots' goods of delivery task participation.

Why social behavior may influence organizational strategy needs to be changed ?

Why any organizations need to know whether nowadays social behaivor how has been changing in order to implement the kind of the most right strategy to achieve the profit aim pursue in possible. I shall indicate nowadays ecommerce or online, customer shopping behavior to explain above question concerns they ought have close relationship between social behavior and organizational strategic choice or organizational behavioral changing need.

On nowadays ecommerce business, or online shopping model, this kind of shopping model in global many young and old age consumers like to apply internet tool to choose any country sellers website stores in order to stay at home to buy any kinds of products from themselves webstores in global societies.

In fact, online shopping model had been popular for long time above to twenty years. Most of global sellers will make decision to design themselves webstores in order to attract global many online buyers to choose to buy their products from themselves webstores. So, it seems that social consumers purchase behaviors had been changed to online shopping from internet invention.

Hence, social consumers purchase behavioral changes may influence any organizations' strategies need to be changed from visiting shops purchase strategy model to online purchase strategy model, if the seller still concentrate on concentrate on considerate how to design itelf , but neglects to considerate how to design itself webstore, e.g. how to design attract product photos to put on itself webstore, how to arrange sale price information location to be putted on webstore and visa card payment location on itself webstore in order to let any one online buyer can feel very easier to buy itself any kinds of products from itself webstore. Then, its potential online buyers will be influenced to increase number when they can find this online seller itself any kinds of products photes and every kinds of product sale price information and visa card payment channel locations easily from itself webstore.

So, it implies that nowadays any one seller ought need to design one webstore to let any one online overseas and domestic consumers can have chance to click itself webstore to choose any one kind of product to buy conveniently when he/she does not hope to leave him/her home to go to shop, because nowadays social shopping behaviors had been influenced to change when internet invention, them it gives another online purchase method to replace visiting shops purchase method to global any one buyer in nowadays societies.

So, if nowadays any one seller still concentrate on how to design itself shop display in order to put any kinds of product on shelf in order to let any one visiting shop customer to find the kind of product to buy, but it neglects to change to choose to pursue another new technological shopping method, such as webstore purchase method in order to implement effective strategy to design the most right webstore as well as in order to attract global overseas and local consumers to find itself webstore easily from website and find its any one kind of product phots and sale price and visa card payment button in order to choose to buy itself any kinds of products in the short time. Consequently I believe that the seller will lose many customers from overseas and local when its other same or similar product sellers choose to design themselves webstores in order to let global any one product buyer can buy themselves any one kind of product when they can pay visa card to buy their products from them webstores conveniently when they stay at home habitly. Then, the seller will lose many global potential customers in long time.

On conclusion, in behavioral economic view, any consumer behavioral social changing, which will influence any in order to avoid customers number loses significantly . In future time, organizations need to make rapid decision in order to implement the most reasonable and the most useful strategy in order to avoid global potential customers number reduces or lose them in long time. So, social behavioral changing environment ought influence any global organizations need to decide how to change themselves strategies in order to avoid customers loses significantly in future time.

How and why human behavior may influence economic growth or recession?

May ourselves daily behaviors influence our global societial continue economic growth or recession? Do they have cause and effect close relationship between human behaviors and global economic growth or recession? I shall apply behavioral economic theory to analyze and explain whether ourselves daily behaviors and our global societial economic growth or recession which have close cause and effect relationship as below:

Every country itself economic development must depend on any business activities, otherwise, any kinds of business activities must need ourselves business activities or behaviors in order to achieve any business activities as well as achieve the country's overall economic development in macro view. However, any country's overall business activites or behaviors which must depend on any kinds of individual businessmen, themselves employees daily working behavior or activity or performance in order to help them to attract or increase many clients number to acieve " earning profit" aim. So, it seems that any individual business, itself overall every department individual working behavior is one main factor to influence the company's overall business performance.

For agricultural fruit and meat food farming industry example, such as New Zealand is a farming main target industry country. It had had many New Zealanders were daily themselves own farming businesses for many years. Their farming businesses include growing fruit, sheep, cow, pig pork, meat etc. food sale business. If the New Zealand farmer owned a large size farming land, then he will choose either growing fruit or feeding sheeps, pigs, cows to be meat to to transport to New Zealand supermarkets to help them to sell to their farmers meet to New Zealanders in order to earn profit. Thus, if the New Zealand farmer owned large size of farming lands, then he needs to employ many farming employees (farming workers) to help him to carry on farming business daily tasks, e.g. picking up friuts, feeding pigs, cows, sheeps to eat food daily. These daily farming jobs are very important to influence this New Zealand farmer's meats or fruits sale number whether they can be easy or diffcult to sell in New Zealand supermarkets , if these farming workers can own encough farming knowledge or skill to know how to pick up fruits method and make judgement to know whether it is right time to pick up the kind of fruits from the trees , as well as know how feed this pigs, sheeps, cows to eat food in order to let they are better health. Consequently, their farming behaviors which can let these animals can provide the best taste and enough meat from these animals to let New Zealander to buy to eat from New Zealand any one supermarket. Even these New Zealand farming workers can know whether the kinds of fruits, e.g. oranges, apples, gapes etc. fruits whether they ought be picked up from the trees at the right time. Consequently, they can make judgement to decide to pick up any kinds of the best taste fruits to let any one New Zealander to buy to eat from any one supermarket in New Zealand. Otherwise, if they do not make judegement to know whether the kind of fruit ought not be picked up because they still need longer time to continue grow up to increase fruit size and better taste from the trees in order to let any one fruit buyer can feel better taste when they eat this kind of fruit later. If they can buy this kind of fruit to eat later, then this New Zealand farmer's his fruit buyers can buy the best taste of this kind of fruit to eat from an yone supermarket in New Zealand. Consequently, many New Zealand supermarkets will choose to buy any kinds of fruits from this farmer fruit supplier when they feel this farmer's fruits can provide more better taste fruits to compare other farmers' fruits.

Thus, due to New Zealand is one farming main income source country. It's any kinds of fruits and meats need to be export to overseas to sell , instead of local sale. It's GDP percent is very high to whole country 's overall income source. So, any one New Zealand farmer individual and any one farming worker individual working behavior will influence its economy whether it is influenced to grow or recession possible. Moreover, it also seems that farming workers' farming knowledge and skill will influence themselves farming daily activities to achieve the aim of the number of increase or decrease to any kinds of fruits whether they are better taste or the number of increase of decrease to any kinds of meats whether they are better taste to supply to any one New Zealand fruit or meat buyers to eat from any one New Zealand supermarket. So, it implies that any one New Zealand farming worker individual farming behavior may influence any kinds of fruits or any kinds of meat taste because they are transported to any one supermarket to sell in New Zealand.

Consequently, if New Zealans had many farmers can teach god farming knowledge and skill to let their any one farming workers know how to decide judgement to decide when it is right time to pick up any kinds of fruits from trees , or how to grow them on soil in order to let they can grow rapidly. Then, many different kinds of fruits can be provided to let any one New Zealanders can eat the best taste of fruits when their fruits are supplied to any one New Zealand supermarkets. Even, if they knew how to feed foods to pigs, cows, sheeps to eat daily. Then they can be more health and they can provide the best taste of meats to let any one New Zealanders can buy their meats from any one New Zealand supermarkets. Moreover, their fruits and meats can be transported to overseas to let any one country fruits or meats buyers can choose any kinds of New Zealand meats and fruits to buy to eat from themselves countries supermarkets. Then, many overseas fruit and meat buyers will perfer to choose New Zealand any kinds of fruits or meats to buy to compare other countries fruits or meats to buy when they go to any one local supermarkets.

On conclusion, it seems that New Zealand farming workers themselves farming behavior may influence their farming employers any kinds of fruits or meats sale number and income because their farming task behaviors must influence whether their fruits or meats taste are the better taste or worse taste to compare their other local farmers (the farmer competitors) whose fruits or meats taste. If tthe farmer's any one farming worker can be trained to learn how to know to feed animals skill and when is the most right time to pick up any kinds of fruits from trees or how to grow them on the soil methods. Due to these farming worker individual farming behavior may influence his different finds of fruits and meats sale number to be increase or decrease, so these any one New Zealand farmer must need to depend on any one farming worker whose farming working methods, if their farming working behaviors can be the best to influence any kinds of fruits to grow rapid or any kinds of pigs, cows, sheeps animals grow up rapidly , then their sale number may be increase significantly and their taste can be improved to let any New Zealand or overseas meat or fruit buyer to buy to eat to feel from any one New Zealand or overseas supermarkets, then New Zealand's agriculture industry must be influenced to increase. In the world, any one fruit or meat buyer must choose to buy New Zealand's fruit and meat to eat in prefer to compare other countries' fruits and meats. So, New Zealand's GDP may be influenced to raise from any one New Zealand farming worker individual farming working behaviors.

Reasons why human behavior may influence economic recession or growth?

Can ourselves daily behaviors or activies influence ourselves countries' economic growth or recession? I shall attempt to explain the reasons why they have direct or indirect relationship between human behavior and economy growth or recession as below:

I shall indicate environment pollution case to attempt to explain above question. Our societies had been experiencing servious environment pollution challenge. However, environment pollution , such as air pollution is caused by air planes and vehicles emission by air planes and vehicles emission as well as water pollution is caused by plastic rubblish, or dirty water or oil or gas chemical material, these both kinds of pollution ought may bring economic recession and this both kinds of pollution are caused by human ourselves daily foolish activities.

I believe human behavior and economy and pollution which have cause and effect relationship. I shall analyze this environment pollution case to explain why they have case and effect relationship between human foolish behavior and environment pollution and economic recession as below:

When global societies had many people like to buy cars to drive to bring emission to fresh air on the roads as well as many manufacturing factories will bring emission to pollute fresh air in their manufacturing processes. Factories and cars will bring air pollution , due to factories need to pollute fresh air in order to manufacture many products and car owners need to drive their cars to go to offices or leisure places. Their cars will also bring emisson to pollute fresh air. On consequence, car owners themselves frequent driving behaviors and factory workers themselves frequent manufacturing behaviors may bring environment pollution. Technology or human behavior whether may influence economic growth or recession. Moreover, air planes also brings emission to pollute air when they are flying in sky. Also, when ships bring oil pollution or sea plastic rubblishs bring pollution to global oceans.

In fact, manufactuers and cars owners, such as factories workers manufacturing behaviours ans car owners driving behaviors and pilots driving air planes flying behaviors and ships transport behaviors, which may cause plastic rubblish, oil or gas emission to sky or sea or on the road to cause ocean and air pollution is serious. However, human ourselves need to buy cars to drive to satisfy ourselves driving leisure or enjoyment, travelers need to catch air planes to travel to enjoy leisure needs, factories workers need help factories to manufacture many products to sell to customers to satisfy their using needs. oil exploration needs to find lands to explore new oil lands.

All of these business and leisure activites may bring serious air and water pollution. However, due to serious air and water pollution will bring earth warming challenge , such as some countries temperature will be influences to rise up to 40 degree or higher br earth warming. However, earth warming is caused by air and ocean pollution. Pollution must be caused by human ourselves, driving cars leisure and factories manufacturing business activities. Hence, if human decided to continue to do these foolish behaviors, we only pursue to manufacture different kinds of industrial products or drive cars to enjoy leisure aims, but we also neglect ourselves behaviors may bring environment pollution. Then, earth warming or earth temperature will be influenced to rise up absolutely in long term. Moreover, if our future earth will be influenced to bring serious high temperature effect by human ourselves these foolish behaviors.

On consequencey, warth warming will bring serious economic losses in possible because when ourselves earth temperature had been influenced to rise up to 40 degree or high. Ourselves health will be caused poor, due to we will feel difficult breath, we must need often tried and hard to work, due to our nervous and health will be influenced to poor by pollution and earth warming effect. Also, we need to pay more money to see doctors when we had long life. Then, our societies will lose may strong labors to help manufacturers to work, e.g. factories will reduce workers number to help manufacturers to produce more different kinds of products, due to workers health is general poor. Due to lacking enough workers to manufacture products, our societies will begin to reduce enough supply number of products to sell to global consumers to satisfy their use needs.

On conclusion, in behaviroal economic view, our societies will lose many labors due to their bodies are not health by air and water pollution. Global economic and business activities will be influenced to worse by global workers reducing number reason. So, economic recession will begin to occur in possible when pollution reaches the serious level.

How employee behavior influences organizational development?

Can any organizational department employee individual behavior may help the organization to bring long term development? When one employee individual behavior, manager won't feel whose task behavior may help organizational development, but when the department has many teams cooperate to work together , all of these team employees whose task behaviors may help their organization to bring long term development.

I shall explain how any why when the organization has many departments, as well as when every team memmber individual behavior may help whole organization to bring long term development in possible as below:

Every organization must need efficient department to cooperate to work together. They may include human resource, finance, logistic, facility management, sales, marketing , operateional , warehouse , factory manufacture , research and development, purchase, customer service etc. different kinds of departments to cooperate to work together. So, any one employee individual behavior, include manager, leader, supervisor, worker, salesperson, manufacture worker, adminisration staff, factory or logistic worker etc. themselves task behavior whether his/her performance is worse or better , whose task behavior ought bring long term good or bad influence to cause the organization's whose efficiency, or performance , whether it can be influenced to improve significantly. For car factory manufacture workers department example, it exmploys 100 car manufacturing workers. They need to manufacture at least 50 cars in order to bring enough car manufacture number to supply to global car buyers to choose to buy (satisfaction to car buyers their driving leisure activity needs). However, if this car manufacture firm employs many low skilful car manufacture workers, their inefficient car skill may bring cars manufacture number reduces, they can not achieve to reach the at least 50 cars manufacture number, if these 100 car manufacture workers. They have half number of workers, they only manufacture 30 to 40 cars number at least daily. So, it seems that this car manufacture firm will have half car manufacture workers bring the low cars manufacture number to compare the another half cars manufacture workers, when this proficient car manufacture workers may manufacture at least 60 or more cars manufacture number daily. So, it explains that this inefficient car manufacture workers will not help this car manufacture company to manufacture enough cars number in order to supply to global car market to sell to satisfy global car buyers needs, when car buyers demand number is more thn car manufacture supply number in supply and demand view. Hence, in long term, if this car manufacture company can not employ new proficient car manufacture workers to replace those inefficient or low skillful car workers. Consequently, its car manufacture number must be influenced to reduce and it can not satisfy global car buyers driving leisure needs.

However, if this car manufacture firm also has shop to sell itself any kinds of cars, instead of manufacturing cars product. So, it needs have both main departments to help it to earn profit. The first step, it needs have proficient car manufacture workers to help it to manufacture at least 50 cars from every car worker in order to have enough cars number to be provided to global car sellers to help it to sell to global car customers. Second step, if it decided to attempt to sell itself cars. Then, it needs to set up car shops in global to different countries in order to let global car buyers may visit its global any one car shop to enquire any one car etc. salesperson about any car quality, speed, gas useful, price, safety, etc. information questions and they can attempt to sit in any one car to feel whether which car can let them to feel more comfortable to make final car purchase decision in any one shop. So, if this car company can provide good sale speaking skillful training to any one car salesperson to let his/her to know whether how to explain every kind of car function and feature, manufacture method etc. questions, then I believe that they can influence any one car buyer to makecar purchase choice decision more easily. So, it this car manufacturer hopes it may attempt to earn profit from different countries car sellers and car buyers both. It ought also provide training course to all general car salespeople to be proficient owning sale speaking skillful professional skill in order to prepare having more confidence to persuade any one car customer to make car purchase choice from any one car salesperson more easily to compare global other car sellers.

Hence, if this car manufacturer could build both car manufacturing team and car sale team more proficient. However, if this car manufacturer hopes to develop itself car manufacture busness to expend to car sale business both in success. It must need to spend long term to provide training courses to general car manufacture workers and general car salespeople both to be proficient car skillful manufacture workers and proficient car skillful salespeople in order to help they can manufacture enough car numbers and help they can persuade may car customers can make car purchase decision in short time when they visit its any one car shop.

However, this car manufacture company explains why every car manufacture worker whose manufacturing behavior and every car salesperson sale persuading speaking ability may help this car manufacture company to expand from its car manufacture market to car sale market development in sussess in possible. So, this car manufacture firm must need these two kinds of essential human resource elements in order to achieve its cars sale number and cars manufacture number increasing aim. They may include proficient car manufacture workers and proficient car salespeople both human resource elements. These both human resource daily task behavior may influence its long term task efficient performance in order to expand itself car sale business in success from itself car manufacture business easily. If it hopes to expand its car manufacture business to car sale business in success. It must need to provide training to these two departments general staffs to be proficient staffs in order to supply enough cars number to its global car shops to let global car buyers can choose its any kinds of cars to buy in any time.

Morevoer, if this car manufacture company can have good skillful of car research and development department , it aims to research and innovate any new technological cars invention in order to improve its any traditional old kinds of cars to be innovative new kinds of cars from every year.

Consequently, its any new innovative cars ought attract global any one car buyer to make car purchase choice final decision more easily, because its any kinds of manufacturng cars can be innovated rapidly to compare its any one car manufacturing competitors, when its nay kinds of cars can be shorten time to innovate within three months, but its any one car manufacturing competitors need to spend more than three months, even one year to innovate themselves traditional old cars products in long term. Hence, its car staffs research and development department staffs must need own good car product design ability, proficient car engineering knowledge , even car invention knowledge in order to innovate its any one kind of car product in short time and introduce to let its global car proficient car buyers feel surprise to its any one kind of innovative car products to compare its any one car manufacturer.Hence, these four departments: car manufacture, car sale and car research and development anr car training departments must need concentrate resource to provide enough training to any one staffs in order to achieve the best performance.

On conclusion, all these departments staffs their performance can influence car manufacture aim to chance to car manufacture and sale aim more significantly. it explains why some main department staffs whole behaviors may influence any organizational performance significantly.

Artificial intelligent Human clever and art creating ability methods

How robots create human clever and art creating ability? Nowadays robots invention may help businesses to reduce employees number, improve performance, raise productivities, reduce cost in service industry,manufacturing industry, office , warehouse, restaurant, hotel , factory, cinema etc. different kinds of business environments, even public transport tools. However, instead of robots may bring these above advantages to any kinds of business working and service environments, whether robots may also help human to create clever and image creating ability. I shall attempt to answer this question:

On the one hand, I believe that past technology ,e.g. machine , it should not have ability to help human to create clever and image creative ability,but nowadays, robots invention that I believe it had had enough ability to help future human to raise more clever and more creating image or painting picture, art design etr. image ability, after robots had been experienced above more than ten years improvement stage from early research stage to invention stage, till to nowadays improvement stage, e.g. non-manual driving auto vehicels, even future non-manual driving skill may be improved to apply to public transport tools, e.g. trams, trains,buses, airplanes, ships etc. public transport tools, when non-manual driving skills can be improved to own the most safe driving skillful ability to compare human driving skills.

On another hand, when robots could be invented to be applied to medical or hospital surgery aspect, e.g. roboting surgerys may help surgery doctors to do complex surgery in surgery rooms, or serving patients tasks in any hospital working environments. They can help nurses and doctors to spend more time to do more important tasks urgently, so medical or surgery serving robots may help nurses and surgery doctors to reduce task load pressure and create clever or improve their surgery skills to when they can cooperate to work in hospitals.

On the other hand, robots can be invented to help any public transport drivers to avoid more traffic accidents occurrence on any countries roads. So, it seems that non-manual driving public transport tools invention may also help human drivers to improve driving skills in possible, when they can learn how to avoid sudden traffic accidents occurrence in any countries roads in any time. so, any kindsof public transport tool drivers ought learn how to avoid traffic accidents skills from future non-manual driving robots invention. Instead of non-manual driving robots and hospital patients medical care or surgery service robots may help public transport tools drivers and hospital nurses and doctors to concentrate on spending time to treat any more important and urgent matters every days. Even, future restaurants may let cooking restaurants may let cooking robots to help human cookers to cook more different kinds of good taste food, to human cookers may learn cooking robots cooking skills in order to improve themselves traditional cooking skills often, in order to compare their cooking skills between human cookers and cooking robots.

On conclusion, it seems that cooking robots ought help human cookers to create any kinds of new cooking skills. Moremove, futuer robot cookers ought be future human cookers their cooking coaches. These robot cookers will help human cookers to create clever cooking skills in possible. Also, future non-manual driving robots ought help human drivers to create new driving skills in order to improve their driving skills to reduce sudden traffic accidents occurrence easily on any countries roads in any time, future hospital surgery or patient care service robots may help surgeons or nurses to do any surgerys in surgery rooms or looking care patients in hospitals. So, when robot surgeons help human surgeons to do complex surgerys in surgerical rooms, human surgeons can learn how to do more complex surgerical tasks for every surgeons when human surgeons can observate every surgerical robots how to do surgeons together. Hence, it seems that robot surgeons also may create future human surgeons themselves innovate surgerical skills from traditional surgerical skills improvement. So, future artificial intelligent technology ought help any kinds of human occupations to create clever, even improvement themselves traditional skills to new innovative skills absolutely.

Why does technology raise online products sale demand and reduces shops products sale demand?

Nowadays robot technology is popular to be applied to different aspects of our daily lives. They may include: non-manual driving vehicles, smart phones, space rockets, kitchen cookers, shopping centres service, cinema ticket sale, etc. different kinds of businesses demand. However, instead of internet invention may influence global communication, media channel is changed to computer internet, media channel is changed to computer internet, media communication from traditional newspaper, letter, TV, radio etc. communication channel. So, any internet users may click to yahoo.com news website to read global news from computer yahoo.com website easily.

In fact, internet technology is also used from businesses. They attempt to set up themselves web stores to sell their products from themselves webstores. So, any one product buyers may buy any kinds of products from any one webstores when they stay at homes. It is very convenient and common to future any one webstore shoppers. It brings this question: Can webstores help online product purchases needs raise and influence shop product purchases need reduce?

In demand and supply view, when one product price raises, its sale demand ought reduce, unless, it can attract to influence customers need consideration or its supply number decreases. But, when one product is increasing sale price to seel from the seller's webstore, whether its sale number will be influenced to reduce. Also, when the kind of product is selling and its sale price is raised, whether it can still keep demand number increase as well as whether it can influence its similar kinds of competitor their products sale demand number to reduce from shop sale channel.

In demand and supply view, when one product price raises, its sale demand ought reduce, unless, it can attract to influence customers need consideration or its supply number decreases. But when one product is increasing sale price to sell from the seller's webstore, whether its sale number will be influenced to reduce. Also, when the kind of product is selling and its sale price is raised, whether it can still keep demand number increases as well as whether it can influence its similar kinds of competitors their products sale demand number to reduce from shop sale channel.

I suppose that webstore sale may influence shop sale demand number decreases, because when internet is popular to use, when one country's buyer wants to buy one kind of product, but he/she can not find the kind of product can be bought from himself/herself home country. If he/she can findthe kind of product to buy from any one of overseas webstore from internet channel at home in any time. Then, he/she will be influenced to make purchase decision from the seller's websote immediately. So, it implies that when on consumer plans to buy one kind of product, he / she will attempt to find the kind of product from any one seller's webstore in preferat home, if he/she spend long time to find the kind of product from many of webstores, but he /she still does not find the kind of product from many of webstores, then he/she will choose to visit any one shop to attempt to buy the kind of product.Hence, online shopping purchase channel will be prefer choice to compare visiting shopd purchase channel in nowadays society.

So, it explains that why the kind of product online sale number may influence the kind of similar product visiting shop sale number either increases or decreases. It means that the kind of product visiting shops sale number may still increases , if the kind of similar products supply number is not enough , they are difficult to let any onc online buyer to find to buy from any one webstore. Otherwise, if the kind of similar products sale supply number is enough to let any one online buyer to find from many webstores. Then, they can influence the similar kinds of shop products purchase demand to reduce and their shops purchase demand will be also influenced to reduce from webstores purchase channel.

On conclusion, it explains that the kind of shop products demand number ought be influenced to increase or decrease, when the similar kind of products can be bought easily from many webstores from internet (e-commerce) shopping channel. Internet (online) technology may help the seller to raise the kind of product competitive ability on purchase demand aspect, when there are not many other sellers can provide webstores to sell the similar kind of products and they only concentrate on selling the kind of similar products from shops to let any one online buyer to frind from may webstores. Then, they can influence the similar kinds of shop products purchase demand to reduce and their shops purchase demand will be also influenced to reduce from webstores purchase channel. Hence, webstore and shop both purchase channel explains that the similar kinds of shop products demand number will be influenced to increase or decrease , when the kinds of product can be bought easily from many webstores from internet shopping channel. Internet technology may help the seller to raise the kind of product competitive ablty to raise purchase demand when there are not many other sellers can provide webstores to sell the kind of similar products and they only concentrate on selling the kind of similar products from shops.

Does car technological development reach mature stage to help economic development?
Our societies had been developing too many years. In our past technological aspect, machine invention had began till to computer invention till to internet invention. It seems that our technological development stage may reach mature stage. Why do I feel our technological development had reached mature stage. I shall apply demand and supply economic theory to explain this question as below:
I shall indicate car development industry to explain whether when car development stage can reach mature stage, it may help global economic growth. In our car technological development stage, it is from gas energy car invention till to nowadays battery energy car invention till to even future non-manual driving car invention. Do you feel that when human (car buyers) felt environmental protecion need to avoid air pollution. So, battery energy cars demand number may increase , it will influence gas energy cars demand number reduces. Even, if future non0manula driving cars invention succeed, lazy driving car buyers will choose to buy non-manual driving (robot driving cars) in preference. So, it is possible that , it will influence future gas energy cars demand number reduces much. I mean that when car buyers can choose many different kinds of non-manual driving cars and battery energy cars to buy. Then, gas energy cars demand number must be influenced to reduce very much as well as gas energy cars supply number will be influenced to reduce to avoid sale prices reduce.
Hence, it explains why future car technological development will reach mature stage when both kinds of non-manual driving cars and battery energy cars are invented to the mature stage. When these two kinds of

cars invention can satisfy future global car buyers driving needs. Then, car maufacturers won't need to spend too much time to continue to attempt to invent any new kinds of cars in order to excite future car buyers' purchase decision. So, I believe that car technological development will reach mature stage within five years, if non-manual driving cars and battery energy cars are invented in success and they can be popular to accept to drive to global car buyers.

On conclusion, when car technological development reaches matural stage, it will help future economy continue grows because when car manufacturers had invented many new kinds of non-manual driving cars and new kinds of non-manual driving cars and new battery energy car sale market. Then, they will encourage or attract global many car buyers choose to buy these both kinds of cars products in preference to compare to traditional gas energy car products. So, they will influence many traditional gas- energy car buyers forgive to drive gas energy cars to avoid non pollution and lazy driving behavioral feeling. So, gas energy car reselling number will increase between gas energy car drivers and past non-owning any car buyers. Also, non-manual driving cars and battery energy car supplying number will be influenced to increase when battery energy car buyers and non-manual driving car buyers driving needs increase.

Consequently, these factors will influence global gas energy cars, non-manual driving cars and battery energy cars their cars purchase and sale transactions increase in future global car market. So, I believe that global car technological development could reach matural stage, then it will infuence global car buyers number increases as well as this car technological mature development stage may also bring global rapid economic growth future non-manual driving car buyers and battery energy car buyers both number increases.

Chapter Explaining supply and demand economic theory

The difference between past and nowadays economists their demand and supply economic theory explanation?

The law of supply and demand defines the relationship between the price of a given good or product and the willingness of people to either buy or sell it. Generally, as the price of a good increases, people are willing to supply more and demand less. These economists had explained economic demand and supply theory as below:

Philosopher John Locke is credited with one of the earliest written descriptions of this economic principle in his 1691 publication, Some

Considerations of the Consequences of the Lowering of Interest and the Raising of the Value of Money. Locke addressed the concept of supply and demand as part of a discussion about interest rates in 17th-century England. Many merchants wanted the government to lower the cap on interest rates charged by private lenders so that people could borrow more money and thus purchase more goods. Locke argued that the free-market economy should set rates because government regulation could have unintended consequences. If the lending industry were left alone, interest rates would regulate themselves, Locke wrote: "The price of any commodity rises or falls by the proportion of the number of buyers and sellers."

Sir James Steuart's Inquiry into the Principles of Political Economy, published in 1796, was the first known printed use of the term "supply and demand." When Steuart wrote his treatise on political economy, one of his main concerns was the impact of supply and demand on laborers.

Adam Smith dealt extensively with the topic in his 1776 epic economic work, The Wealth of Nations. Often referred to as the Father of Economics, Smith explained the concept of supply and demand as an "invisible hand" that naturally guides the economy. According to Smith, the invisible hand is the automatic pricing and distribution mechanisms in the economy. Smith described a society in which bakers and butchers provide products that individuals need and want, providing a supply that meets demand and developing an economy that benefits everyone. It is important to note that Smith's ideas haven't gone without critique over the years since his ideas were first published, though. Over time, his ideas have been added to in order to represent the changing times and include concepts such as marginal utility, comparative advantage, entrepreneurship, the time-preference theory of interest, and monetary theory.

One of Marshall's most important contributions to microeconomics was his introduction of the concept of price elasticity of demand, which examines how price changes affect demand. In theory, people buy less of a particular product if the price increases, but Marshall noted that in real life, this behavior was not always true. The prices of some goods can increase without reducing demand, which means their prices are inelastic. Inelastic goods tend to include items such as medication or food that consumers deem crucial to daily life. Marshall argued that supply and demand, costs of production, and price elasticity all work together.

Nowadays economists they explain demand and supply economic theory, they have some different to past economists whose explanation as below:

How Does Supply and Demand Work? The law of supply and demand is a theory that explains the interaction between the sellers of a resource and the buyers of that resource. Generally, as price increases, people are willing to supply more and demand less and vice versa when the price falls. What does the bottom line mean. Despite the origins of the law of supply and demand beginning hundreds of years ago, it's still a topic frequently referenced and utilized today in economic theory and discussions. The theory has developed over time to accommoda

Explaining supply and demand economic theory

The difference between past and nowadays economists their demand and supply economic theory explanation?

The law of supply and demand defines the relationship between the price of a given good or product and the willingness of people to either buy or sell it. Generally, as the price of a good increases, people are willing to supply more and demand less. These economists had explained economic demand and supply theory as below:

Philosopher John Locke is credited with one of the earliest written descriptions of this economic principle in his 1691 publication, Some Considerations of the Consequences of the Lowering of Interest and the Raising of the Value of Money. Locke addressed the concept of supply and demand as part of a discussion about interest rates in 17th-century England. Many merchants wanted the government to lower the cap on interest rates charged by private lenders so that people could borrow more money and thus purchase more goods. Locke argued that the free-market economy should set rates because government regulation could have unintended consequences. If the lending industry were left alone, interest rates would regulate themselves, Locke wrote: "The price of any commodity rises or falls by the proportion of the number of buyers and sellers."

Sir James Steuart's Inquiry into the Principles of Political Economy, published in 1796, was the first known printed use of the term "supply and demand." When Steuart wrote his treatise on political economy, one of his main concerns was the impact of supply and demand on laborers.

Adam Smith dealt extensively with the topic in his 1776 epic economic work, The Wealth of Nations. Often referred to as the Father of Economics, Smith explained the concept of supply and demand as an "invisible hand" that naturally guides the economy. According to Smith, the invisible hand is the automatic pricing and distribution mechanisms in the economy. Smith described a society in which bakers and butchers provide products that individuals need and want, providing a supply that meets demand and developing an economy that benefits everyone. It is important to note that Smith's ideas haven't gone without critique over the years since his ideas were first published, though. Over time, his ideas have been added to in order to represent the changing times and include concepts such as marginal utility, comparative advantage, entrepreneurship, the time-preference theory of interest, and monetary theory.

One of Marshall's most important contributions to microeconomics was his introduction of the concept of price elasticity of demand, which examines how price changes affect demand. In theory, people buy less of a particular product if the price increases, but Marshall noted that in real life, this behavior was not always true. The prices of some goods can increase without reducing demand, which means their prices are inelastic. Inelastic goods tend to include items such as medication or food that consumers deem crucial to daily life. Marshall argued that supply and demand, costs of production, and price elasticity all work together.

Nowadays economists they explain demand and supply economic theory, they have some different to past economists whose explanation as below:

How Does Supply and Demand Work? The law of supply and demand is a theory that explains the interaction between the sellers of a resource and the buyers of that resource. Generally, as price increases, people are willing to supply more and demand less and vice versa when the price falls. What does the bottom line mean. Despite the origins of the law of supply and demand beginning hundreds of years ago, it's still a topic frequently referenced and utilized today in economic theory and discussions. The theory has developed over time to accommodate recent technological and economical advancements, but the basic ideas of the theory remain largely the same.

Does demand depend on supply?

Supply and Demand Determine the Price of Goods and Quantities Produced and Consumed. Consumers may exhaust the available supply of a good by purchasing a given good or service at a high volume. This leads to an increase in demand. As demand increases, the available supply also decreases.

What does market demand depend on?

Market factors affecting demand of consumer goods. The demand for a good increases or decreases depending on several factors. This includes the product's price, perceived quality, advertising spend, consumer income, consumer confidence, and changes in taste and fashion.

Who controls the demand in supply and demand?

Supply and demand are in turn determined by technology and the conditions under which people operate. At one extreme, the market could be populated by a large number of virtually identical sellers and buyers (for example, the market for ballpoint pens).

What are the two laws of demand and supply?

The law of demand holds that the demand level for a product or a resource will decline as its price rises, and rise as the price drops. Conversely, the law of supply says higher prices boost supply of an economic good while lower ones tend to diminish it.

What factors affect demand and supply?

Price fluctuations are a strong factor affecting supply and demand. When a product gets expensive enough that the average consumer no longer feels it is worth it to buy the product, then the demand declines. This leads to cuts in production that will hopefully stabilize the product's value.

What factors affect demand and demand?

Demand may be defined as the quantity of a commodity that a consumer is able and willing to buy, at each possible price, over a given period of time. ● Essential elements of demand are quantity, ability, willingness, prices, and period of time.

Which factors affect supply?

Generally, the supply of a product depends on its price and other variables such as the cost of production.

a. Price. Price can be understood as what the consumer is willing to pay to receive a good or service. ...

b. Cost of production. ...

c. Technology. ...

d. Governments' policies. ...

e. Transportation condition.

How does supply and demand work together?

It's a fundamental economic principle that when supply exceeds demand for a good or service, prices fall. When demand exceeds supply, prices tend to rise. There is an inverse relationship between the supply and prices of goods and services when demand is unchanged.

What happens to supply when demand increases?

An increase in demand, all other things unchanged, will cause the equilibrium price to rise; quantity supplied will increase. A decrease in demand will cause the equilibrium price to fall; quantity supplied will decrease.

What is the theory of demand?

Demand theory describes the way that changes in the quantity of a good or service demanded by consumers affects its price in the market, The theory states that the higher the price of a product is, all else equal, the less of it will be demanded, inferring a downward sloping demand curve.

What are the 4 basic laws of supply and demand?

1) If the supply increases and demand stays the same, the price will go down. 2) If the supply decreases and demand stays the same, the price will go up. 3) If the supply stays the same and demand increases, the price will go up. 4) If the supply stays the same and demand decreases, the price will go down.

The different types of demand are as follows:

i. Individual and Market Demand: ...

ii. Organization and Industry Demand: ...

iii. Autonomous and Derived Demand: ...

iv. Demand for Perishable and Durable Goods: ...

v. Short-term and Long-term Demand:

What creates demand for a product?

You can create demand for a unique product if you can manage to solve a persistent problem for the consumer. People are always running away from pain, and providing them with an outlet is a sure-fire way to create massive demand for your goods.

What are the 7 factors that affect supply?

The seven factors which affect the changes of supply are as follows: (i) Natural Conditions (ii) Technical Progress (iii) Change in Factor Prices (iv) Transport Improvements (v) Calamities (vi) Monopolies (vii) Fiscal Policy.

What can affect demand?

Factors Affecting Demand

Price of the Product. ...

The Consumer's Income. ...

The Price of Related Goods. ...

The Tastes and Preferences of Consumers. ...

The Consumer's Expectations. ...

The Number of Consumers in the Market.

What are the three factors affecting demand?

The demand for a product will be influenced by several factors:

Price. Usually viewed as the most important factor that affects demand. ...

Income levels. ...

Consumer tastes and preferences. ...

Competition. ...

Fashions.

What are the 4 factors of supply?

The four factors that can shift the supply curve include natural conditions, input prices, technology, and government.

What causes increase in supply?

If the cost of production is lower, the profits available at a given price will increase, and producers will produce more. With more produced at every price, the supply curve will shift to the right, meaning an increase in supply.

What causes supply changes?

A change in supply is an economic term that describes when the suppliers of a given good or service alter production or output. A change in supply can occur as a result of new technologies, such as more efficient or less expensive production processes, or a change in the number of competitors in the market.

Is supply and demand a good strategy?

When it comes to profit placement, supply and demand zones can be a great tool as well. Always place your profit target ahead of a zone so that you don't risk giving back all your profits when the open interest in that zone is filled.

How is demand created?

Demand creation is a process that fuels the revenue pipeline so the sales team can meet or exceed their quotas. In other words, it takes your big idea — the creative appeal of your brand — and turns it into sales. That sounds a lot like demand generation, which often gets confused with lead generation.

What are the two parts of demand?

Economists define demand as the quantity of a good or service that buyers are willing and able to buy at all possible prices during a certain time period. Notice that there are two components to demand: willingness to purchase and ability to pay.

Can we control demand?

If you're willing to think and act strategically, you can easily manipulate the laws of supply and demand. It should be surprising to learn, however, that by manipulating the laws of supply and demand, you can make more profit in less time and with far fewer headaches

How do you control demand?

Here are five short-term actions to improve your demand variability management plans in this time of uncertainty:

Maintain transparent, proactive relationships with your suppliers. ...

Activate alternate sources of supply. ...

Reduce lead times. ...

Update inventory policy and planning. ...

Align supply and demand management.

What are the 8 types of demand?

There are 8 states of demand: negative demand, no demand, latent demand, falling demand, irregular demand, full demand, overfull demand and unwholesome demand.

What is Demand?

Types of Determinants of Demand. Every factor has a unique impact on demand. ...

Price of the Product. ...

The Income of the Consumers. ...

Number of Buyers in the Market. ...

Consumer's Expectations. ...

Tastes and Preferences of The Consumers. ...

Complement Goods. ...

Substitute Product.

What is theory of supply?

The law of supply is a fundamental principle of economic theory which states that, keeping other factors constant, an increase in price results in an increase in quantity supplied. In other words, there is a direct relationship between price and quantity: quantities respond in the same direction as price changes.

What are the types of supply?

There are five types of supply—market supply, short-term supply, long-term supply, joint supply, and composite supply.

Which comes first supply or demand?

Demand comes first and it's followed by the corresponding supplies. Supply and demand are both very important to economic activity. Supply is the total amount of a particular good or service available at a given time to consumers at a given price. Demand is a representation of a consumer's desire to purchase goods and services; it acts as a measurement of a consumer's willingness to purchase a specific good or service at a given price. These two economic forces influence each other; they are both important for the economy because they impact the prices of consumer goods and services within an economy and the quantities produced and consumed. Supply and demand are both keys to understanding the economy because they reflect the prices and quantities of consumer goods and services within an economy.

What are the relationship between demand and supply?
According to market economy theory, the relationship between supply and demand balances out at a point in the future; this point is called the equilibrium price.
Economists and companies analyze the relationship between supply and demand when making strategic product decisions. Both economists and companies analyze the relationship between supply and demand when making strategic product decisions. The assumption behind a market economy is that supply and demand are the best determinants for an economy's growth and health.
Consumer Behavior Influences Demand
One way that companies or economists might analyze this relationship is to create graphs that chart the equilibrium price of certain goods and services in order to determine product development and their production schedule. Consumer behavior dictates which products are produced and sold because consumers create the demand that companies attempt to meet. As a result, companies may study consumer behavior in an attempt to understand the current demand and predict future demand. It is vital that companies maintain the capacity to produce enough of a good or service that they can satisfy consumer demands.
Supply and demand are two sides of the same market coin. Generally, supply is how much of something is available or will be produced at a certain price. Demand is how much of something people want to purchase or consume at a certain price. One way to develop a more precise relationship between the two is to consider how the price of something affects its supply and its demand. Generally when the price of a good goes up, so does the supply, since firms are willing to create more when they can

sell at higher prices. But when the price of a good goes up consumers will, at the same time, generally demand less. It is the interaction of supply and demand that determines how much will be produced and consumed and at what price, converging to a state known as equilibrium.

CHAPTER FIVE

Technology how influences consumer demand changes

Face reading technology and video camera recording consumer behavior predictive differences

● Recommendation of face reading technology is for confectionery food manufacturers at factory or office experiment and ethnographic consumer behavior video camera recording method is for product manufacturers at home

● Abstract

The impact of emotions on judges, evaluations and decisions have long been important to psychology and consumer behavior on consumption. I shall examine how distinct perspectives shape the processes of appraisal that lead to emotional experience and how different consumers might define happiness distinctly. I examine emotions that vary by positive, negative and mixed. I also suggest new ways to distinguish among emotions and to assess how new ways to consumers to aim to be discovered by better understanding how consumers manage their experience of emotion to achieve their own affective goals. In my report, I shall indicate three aspects to research. The first aspect, I indicate how one sample technology to detect consumer emotion to predict facial reaction, such as Noldus Face Reader technology is used orange juice, sweets and chocolates confectionery foods or drinks to detect young consumers' emotion whether who like or dislike to eat or drink different brands of confectionery products from whose facial reaction for factory or shop experiments. Besides, how to use video cameras to record consumer individual behavior at home to predict why who choose to buy your product to help manufacturer, as you to predict why your clients choose to buy your products or choose not to buy products to use.

● Main Problem Being Addressed of face reading and video camera technology limits

Technologies that detect consumers' emotions can help companies to reduce the amount of money waste on unsuccessful product launches by stopping products before they are launched. Methods can be accurately measured consumers' feelings and emotion for a food or beverage product irrespective of consumer's ability to accurately articulate those feelings are needed in order to generate more accurate food and beverage product testing results. These methods will be based on the measurement of human physiology-most likely facial expressions, but they reveal intentionally hidden or subconscious emotions. In addition, the method may be able to decide emotions: Such as happiness, sadness, surprise, fear, anger feeling when one youth person eats a food or drinks beverage product. The first aspect main problem concerns how face reading technology can be measured to predict consumer acceptance level of confectionery foods or soft drinks from their face expression in the short time more absolutely. However, this face reading technology can't be used to predict any consumer's individual enjoyable acceptance satisfactory level when who uses any manufacturer's products in the short time.So face reading technology can not be used to predict any consumer's emotion to reflect to use any product more easily.

Thus, I shall recommend how to use video camera recording ethnographic research method to find what factors to influence the consumer who decides to buy the product to use and evaluate whose satisfactory level to use the product at home. I concern how to use video camera to predict consumer individual behavioral process to find why who choose to buy the kind of product to evaluate the most absolute emotion response to find whether who satisfies or doesn't satisfy to use the product. Also how to use face reading technology to measure different level sugar elements to add the confectionery foods to detect the consumer's emotion whether who likes or does not like to eat the kind of confectionery food.

● Summary of ethnographic research
of facial reading technology and video camera technology

To detect consumer's emotion like or not like to eat the
confectionery foods, e.g. soft orange juice, sweet and
chocolates. The food manufacturer may attempt to use face reading technology to predict different level sugar elements to add its confectionery

eating products to see consumer's different face impression to evaluate whether what sugar elements , e.g. how much weights are the suitable level to add to the kind of confectionery food. To detect buyer's emotion whether who enjoy or does not enjoy to use the manufacturer's product and to find what factor(s)can influence the consumer to choose to buy the product. The home product manufacturer may use digital cameras and computer recording method to record the volunteer daily routines filmed at home. It aims to detect consumer's individual using behavior to research whether what psychological factors are to influence who to choose to buy themanufacturer's product to use. Otherwise, Ethnographic research concerns how to use video camera to record consumers' behavior daily about one weeks. It aims to predict what factors case who to buy the kind of product. Hence, Confectionery manufacturers can use face reading technology to predict consumer emotion of satisfactory level to eat sweats, ice creams, chocolates, biscuits etc. sugar add confectionery. Home product manufacturers can use video camera technology to predict consumer emotion of satisfactory level to use products at home e.g. clothing, radios, televisions, furniture, sleeping beds etc. home daily useful products.

● Comparative Benefits / Advantages

Face reading technology can help only confectionery eating food manufacturers to measure sugar element whether how much sugar weights are the most suitable to young people taste acceptable level more absolutely. Digital camera and computer recording technology can predict whether what factors can influence the consumer to choose to buy your competitor's similar product or your products and measure whose satisfactory level to let manufacturer to judge how to manufacture whose products of features are more suitable to be acceptable or attractive to consumers' taste.

If the confectionery eating food manufacturer could not detect consumers' emotion to know whether what level of sugar ingradient is the most suitable level to cause who are like or dislike to eat or drink confectionery foods from whose face expression absolutely. It will be serious loss to invest time and money to manufacture this foods and consumers will feel their foods or soft drinks is not health to eat to cause illness possibly. Traditional sensory and consumption tests predict consumer acceptance of new food products rather poorly, as are evidenced by the high their failure rates in the market. These tests typical reflect conscious processes whereas consumer acceptance may also be based on unconscious processes. For example, I feel functional (MFR) isn't an allowable technology space primarily due to consumer concern of manipulation. Miller (2012) indicated that " functional MRI mind reading technology is where something is wholly subjective and private, and it can't be predict consumer emotion to tell from what who're doing or looking at, what whose mental state is." Hence, It has a distinction between that kind of mind reading and what is brain reading, which essentially involves using brain scans to figure out what the factors can influence on consumer's mind in different situations to decide buy or not buy the food product. So, any consumer emotion researcher needs to wait a few seconds to see what consumers will do next. The technology is still limited, such as individual differences: Different consumers' brains code information sight differently, so consumer emotion researcher needs to learn how a specific individual codes consumers' emotion mental states. How to produce the most acceptable sugar level to manufacture any confectionery eating food or drink for children, it can keep consumers who will choose to buy other brands of confectionery eating food or drink more easily. This is the most important factor to influence your children taste choice to feel your brand confectionery eating food or drink is the best taste to compare other brand competitors. So, sugar ingradient (element) of the acceptable level is the most important research from face reading technology experiment in shop or factory.

The Netherlands (2014) indicated "Arnade had been carring to investigate consumers (man age 22 years) were recruited at the kaunas University of Technology. They were asked to rate the sample and then are characterized by Face reader program (Naldus Information Technology) Wageningen. The measurements are showed significant differences between facial expressions by the different samples of tested sugar element confectionery products and reflected liking ratings well. The positive correlations of facial expression happy and negative correlations of sad expression are predicted. It suggested that these may be the most valuable descriptors for explaining the quality of sweets and chocolates. It can be concluded that Noldus face reader technology is sufficiently accurate for differentiating between sugar confectionery products and can deliver additional information to conventional acceptance tests. " Otherwise, reasons for likes or dislikes of different foods or drinks are typically difficult to articulate, but may determine much of our food or drinks choice. Certain foods or drinks can be more active than other foods or drinks because for some reason who make consumers feel good when their express positive emotion. Arnade (2014) examined "consumers' facial reaction by the flavor of orange juice drinks using face reader technology measurement showed significant differences between facial expressions by the different samples. The explicit measurement reflected the liking ratings well. Especially expressions happy with liking and were good indicators for liked and liked samples respectively, 20 minimize artefacts, caused by the face reader software as emotion, they used liquid samples (juice) which need less processing in the mouth than solid samples." The aim of this work was to examine whether facial expressions measured with the Noldus face reader technology are a sufficiently accurate measure for differentiating between various types of sugar element confectionery including sweets, chocolates and juice drinks or soft drinks which need sugar element to add in the manufacturing processing and to investigate whether facial reactions are able to explain such these confectionery foods or drinks liking ratings.

The impact of emotions on judge , evaluations and decisions has long been important to psychology and consumer behavior on consumption. It seems face reading technology can predict whether the consumer likes or dislikes these confectionery foods, chocolates, sweets or juice, soft drinks liking ratings to measure whether sugar element is excess or less from young consumers' face expression, such as enjoying or not enjoying of feeling, smile or no smile response. Hence, face measuring technology can be more difficult to detect consumers 'emotion for product manufacturer. Because consumers need to spend more time to attempt to use their new innovative products.

● Recommendation Ethnographic consumer behavior research is for video camera recording to product manufacturers at home

Otherwise, it seems product manufacturers can't use face reading technology to detect consumers' emotion in the short time immediately. The products include any kind of products, e.g. high technological products, such as space mining of resources machines, satellite navigation system ,cars , machines etc. as well as home useful technological electronic products, such as mobile phones, washing machines, televisions, laptops as well as daily products, such as shirts, shoes, furniture, toys, tooth pastes etc. These essential home product and high technologic product manufacturers who need to continue to innovate their old style products to follow consumers' taste to invent new style products to be accepted to their fresh taste.

It seems that manufacturers need to spend a long time to touch consumers' feeling whether whose old style technological products which are still accepted to them to use or not. Hence, it implies that a consumer decides to buy these high technological innovation products, whose choice isn't performed to show who must accept to use these high technological innovation productsfor long time, whose emotion is not sure whether who feels satisfactory to consume to use this product for a long time. When he/she uses this technological product for a long time, it is possible that who will feel it was not valuable to buy it before. Hence, video camera can used to record the consumer's behavior record whose image and to analyze whose facial expressions and bodily gestures at home about one week.

● How to use video camera recording to predict consumer's emotion . How to use automated facial expression analysis for emotion and behavior prediction. The expression of emotion is achieved through combinations of verbal and nonverbal information produced from various sources of the body and the brains. Nonverbal information encompasses any message that is not expressed in words, including gestures, postures to be performed from individual behavior for individual daily life. Though people often don't invest much thought to the nonverbal aspect of communication to be performed to manage emotional experiences. Computers enable researchers to process to gather data in a short amount of time to predict facial expression consumers. The new methodological for social scientists may be a valid analysis to automated facial expression from consumer's daily behavior at home experiement for several days investigation more absolutely. Among the various models of nonverbal communication, we focus on facial expression which are captured by small digital cameras and later analyzed with computer software.

As Webb et. al. (2000) pointed out, "people are low-fidelity observational instruments recording and interpretation may be erratic over time, as the observer learns and responds to the research phenomena he or she observes. It means that we can observe consumer behavior to predict why who buy the product from whose daily life behavior performance. Recent studies applied automated feature extraction and classification to extract macro features . Such as the head and hand position and angle from video features taken during an experiment where a theft took place. It also implied that computer models obtained up to 71 percent correct classification of innocent or guilty participants based on the macro features extracted from the video camera. Furthermore, in an overview of detection research." Meservy et al.(2008) noted that "the accuracy of humans coding behavioral indicators only falls around 50 percent, but that computers trained to a automatically extract and identify relevant behavioral cues detect deception with significantly higher accuracy. Furthermore, computers operate without the other methods(e.g. physiological measures such as polygraph machines or lie detectors) and the lost of extensively trained human interviewers.''

Ambady and Rosenthal (1992) showed that ''another advantage of why automated facial detection technology coupled with computational models is that once the system secures the parameters for a model, prediction of behavior (vs simple detection and classification) can be made using only a small sample. This is a computational recording of what social psychologists, a way people sample a short except from social behavior to draw inferences of about states, traits and other personally relevant characteristics .For instance, based on an observation of a three minute video clip of a conflict between a married couple.''

Carrere and Gottman(1999) also indicated ''video cameras were able to predict the outcome of that marriage after six years. Using machine learning coupled with computer vision allows computers to cause this human cognitive process; models are trained on a short sample of facial features and those features automatically predict future behaviors. Computers were used in place of human coders to detect vocal behaviors (e.g. time spent speaking, influence over conversation partners, variation in pitch and volume and behavior mirroring) during a negotiation task. Their results imply that the speech features extracted during the first five minutes of negotiation are highly predictive of future outcomes.'' The researchers also noted that using computers to code speech features offers advantages such as high test-retest reliability and real time feedback. As a cost-effective and relatively accurate method to detect, track and create models for behavior classification and prediction, automatic facial expression analysis has the potential to be applied to multiple disciplines. Capturing behavioral data from participants may be a more accurate representation of how and what they feel, and a better alternative to self-report questionnaires that interrupt participants' affective cognitive processes and are subject to bias .Our model goes beyond to predict the future behavior within a given task (e.g. a virtual car accident or an error in performance). This opens up the possibility of such models becoming a common methodology in social scientific and behavioral research.

Installing video camera recording at sample consumers to carry on investigating their feeling to use their product to collect the more truly acceptable or not acceptable feeling to use the product reason, such as: video camera recording method is data synchronization and time series statistics calculation. In the next phase of analysis, video recording are recording with data collected from experimental tasks such as surveys or simple motor tasks. This is done to map the extracted facial geometry information to behavioral output data. In the experiments three to five second intervals of facial expressions were taken one to two seconds before each instance of the behavior to be predicted and used as the input data. After data synchronization we also computed a series of time-domain statistics on coordinates in each interval to use as additional inputs to our classifiers. For example one sample investigating. The input data for this study consisted of videotapes of forty one participants watching films that elicited the emotions of either amusement or sadness, along with measures of their cardiovascular activity responding. It should be noted that the recorded expressions were expressions, unlike the photographs of deliberately posed faces often used in prior facial expression research. However, I suggest these entertainment product or home product manufacturers who can use video cameras to record whose buyers' behavior to detect whose emotion to aim to design which kind of colors, styles, sizes and how to change whose old products' features to attract the more consumers' fresh demand taste .

Ethnographic research is interpretative research which seeks an understanding from the perspectives of the value systems of those being researched. Ethnographic search is one different method to learn about buyer individual behavior to compare with enquiring questionnaires to participants to fill to answer questions to gather data to carry on the sale and post purchase evaluation cycle to evaluate whether what are their product criteria or weaknesses which need to improve to raise their sale competition in their market.

Palmer (2012) reported " one sport shoe company's ethnographic research in action was provided by a product commissioned by the footwear brand Dr Martens. It aims to research how to understand young people's buying behavior. It wanted to understand how youth people used brands in their every lives. Why for example, did some brands , such as Nike trainers or baseball caps become popular in youth culture? The researchers identified groups of young people around the world who responded to Dr Marten's target market. In return for a payment, volunteers were followed for several days and their daily routines filmed with a handheld digital camera. In total, 180 hours of captured film was edited to just one hour of highlights showing the key drivers of youth culture which are relevant to the Dr Martens brand. It seems that young people preferred fashions that allowed them to customize an item of clothing and in some way take ownership of it. The research drew the conclusion that iconic fashion items for young people had to have a distinctive label or style that made their wearers stand out as part of a tribe." Hence, ethnographic research seems to help this company to know why the young clients choose to buy those brands sport shoes, it is possible that the these brands sport shoes' color or design can be accepted more to them to buy Dr Marten brand's sport shoes when they wear different style of clothing. Hence, it uses digital cameras to observe the worldwide choice of paying target youth volunteers whose daily individual behaviors at homes to get the more actual evidence to evaluate what factors influence youth clients choose to buy these brands of sport shoes. It seems this sport shoe company can take several hours of filming to yield just a few moments of true insights to participant's true attitudes and behavior.

Ethnography is one of many approaches that can be found within Social research. Ethnography was a descriptive account of a commonly or culture. Ethnography usually involves the researcher participating in people's daily lives for an extended period of time, watching what happens, listening to what is said, and/or asking questions through informal and formal interviews collecting documents. In more detailed terms, ethnographic work usually has most of the following features: People actions are studied in every contexts rather than under conditions created by the researcher, in experimental or high structured interview situations as well as data are gathered for a range of sources including documentary evidence of various kinds, but participant observation and/or relatively informal conversations are main ones as well as data collected is for the most past relatively unstructured in two senses and it doesn't involve following through detailed research design at the start and the categories that are used for interpreting what people say or are not built into the data collection process through the use of observation schedules or questionnaires to analyze.

Generally, fairly small scale perhaps a style setting or group of people. This is a facilitate in depth study and analysis of data involves interpretation of the meaning, functions and consequences of human actions and low are implicated in local and perhaps also wider contexts what are produced for the most part are verbal descriptions, explaining and theories and statistical analysis play a subordinate role at most. How ethnography can learn more about buyer behavior to help product manufacturers to detect consumers' emotion. It means collection of data to pursue an answers to these questions more effectively and to test those against evidence. Hence, video camera recording to consumer's individual useful behavior at whose home. It isn't set up for research purposes (such as experiments or formal interviews). The methodological model for social research is physical science conceived in terms of the logic of the experiment. However, ethnography was sometimes dismissed as quite inappropriate to social science on the grounds that data and findings it produces are subjective. Hence, ethnographic research is the role to learn more about buyer behavior through marketers may have been listening more to consumers (e.g. through qualitative research), efforts have almost always been directed at controlling consumers ranges of products or services predetermined by producers have been pushed through with littler real involvement of consumers in the process at a time in which consumers are ever more aware of what is being done to marketers. To seeing consumer's daily life behavior can predict why who choose to buy your or your competitor's product. Then, the product manufacturer can judge what the reasons are caused to attract the consumer chooses to buy the product to use. Hence, the data analysis procedure will include these steps as below:

● First step, Facial expression videos camera record activity ; input data from given tasks will be carrying on researching at the same time.

● Second step, the feature extraction will be caused

● Third step, the chi-square feature selection will be caused

● Fourth step, the machine learning training will be caused

● The final step, the results of behavioral prediction and data classification will be output at the same time.

● Why ethnographic research can be predicted consumer's behavioral performance to detect emotion by video recording camera at home ?
Ethnographic field research involved the study of groups and people as go about every day lives. There has two distinct activities. First the ethnographer enter into a social setting and gets to know the people and observes all the approach. But second the ethnographer writes down regular systematic ways what who observes and learns when participating in the quality rounds of life of others. Thus, the researcher creates an accumulating written records of these observations and experiences. Two interconnected activities comprise the care of ethnographic search:

participation in some initially familiar social world and the production of written accounts of that world by drawing upon such participation. Hence, ethnographers are committed to get close to the activities and everyday people. Getting close minimally requires physical and social proximity to the daily rounds of people lives and activities, the field researcher must be able to take up positions in order observe and understand whom.

Consumer behavior refers to the behavior that consumers display in searching for purchasing , using , evaluating and disposing of products and services that who expect will satisfy their needs and it's behaviors that are directly involved in the action of obtaining, consuming and spending products or services, including the decision processes that precede and follow these actions. It seems ethnographic research can helps the marketer to understand how consumer think, feel and select from alternative like products, brands and the like and how the consumers' buying behaviors are influenced by their environment, the reference group, family and salespersons.

Consumer buying behavior includes that: Attitude itself is a learning experience and can lead to a change in attitude before buyers enter the buying process. Thus, attitude don't automatically guarantee all types of behavior. Attitudes based on behavioral learning follow beliefs, behaviors and effect sequence. A consumer who is high involved with a product or service category and who perceives a high level of product or service differentiation between alternatives with follow the cognitive hierarchy (belief affect behavior). From the ethnographic research marketers perspective the sequence of attitude formation is from a communication point of views from a strategic point of view, such as it has proved useful in specifying the different elements that work to influence buyers' evaluations of attitude, product or services may be composed of attributes or qualities, some of which may be more important than others to particular people. So consumer's individual decision is to act on whose attitudes is affected by other factors, such as whether it is felt other factors, such as whether it is felt that buying a product or service would be met with approval by friends and family.

According to this approach, ethnographic research marketers must concentrate an assessing the characteristics of the environment, such as the physical surroundings and product or service placement, that influence members of that target market. Such as point of purchase (such as selling the sport shoe brand's some sample of design style shoes) are particularly useful in predicting to find reasons why individual consumer choose to buy these styles. Hence, I recommend ethnographic research marketers can focus on measuring consumers' effective emotion response to products or services and develop offering that elicit appropriate subjective reactions and employ effective symbolism to predict how the different brand products to be designed which kind of style, to be used what kinds of colors and what kinds of materials to be produced.

To decide which is the most acceptance to satisfy consumers' taste. Such as the above sport shoe brand company case showed that it attempted to use ethnographic method to research whether what the external or internal factors are influenced to the footwear brand Dr martens' other consumers to choose the Nike or Baseball brands sport shoes to buy. It discovered that what youth people whose daily wearing clothing colors, designs and materials external factors which can influence them to choose to buy which kinds of design styles, colors and materials made of sport shoes to buy. It seems famous brands of sport shoes and cheaper price and durability internal factors are not the important factors to influence them to choose to buy these brands. Otherwise, the youth people whose wearing clothing colors, design styles and material made external factors can influence their feeling to choose the most adaptable style of sport shoes to be accepted to adapt to accept to their wearing clothing fashion. Thus, it seems that ethnographic research is one good method to detect consumers emotion whether the individual consumer's choice is influenced by the product's internal factors more or external environment external factors more to influence every individual consumer to feel positive or negative emotion to make final decision to buy any product to use possibly. If the product manufacturer can use this ethnographic research method to attempt to find whether what external or internal factors can influence potential consumers' fashion acceptance level to choose to buy any new innovative products to predict their emotion before the new peoduct manufacturer decides to manufacture its products to sell in this competitive market. I believe that its predicting market success chance will be increased.

constructive consumer choice process

● How constructive consumer choice process measures which attribute factor(s) can influence consumer chooses to buy any product or food in psychological view.

● Main Problem Being Addressed

The second aspect problem is judged whether constructive consumer choice is an important process to influence any consumer to choose to buy any products. If it is a real essential choice process, how product manufacturers can reduce their negative emotion is caused to choose not buy their products during this constructive process. The second aspect main problem is researched about consumer will choose to make final decision to buy the best choice of product from among brands of products . Hence, the constructive consumer choice process is a real essential choice process to any consumer generally, when individual consumer needs to compare different brands of products to choose to buy any product.

How product manufacturers can predict whose choice method to decide to prefer to make final decision to buy any products in the short days or the short time in the constructive consumer process. If manufacturers can know overall consumers' choice method, manufacturers will not design the not suitable style of products to manufacture to sell and who can know what the overall consumers' negative emotion is influenced who decide not to buy their products from their design style in order to manufacture more suitable style of product design . I shall recommend how manufacturers can predict consumer emotion in the constructive consumer choice process in psychological view.

My research is concerned knowledge opinion about how to predict consumer emotion whether what attribute factor(s)
are the most influence to the consumer to choose to buy the
manufacturer's product in whose process of choice. If manufacturer can early know whether what the most attractive attribute factor(s) are the most influence to the consumer to decide to buy whose product, so who can concentrate on manufacturing the different kinds of products to get the most influence attribute factor to attract consumers to choose to buy whose products. Hence, the manufacturer can know what reasons can cause the consumers who do not choose to buy its products during constructive consumer choice process generally , who can know how to improve its product's design method to concentrate on producing the most acceptable satisfactory level to sell to whose consumers in .Also I believe that the manufacturer can raise sale numbers if who know what bad factors to cause whose consumers choose not to buy whose products during the constructive consumer choice process. It can increase chance to change its product innovative strategy to raise confidence to judge what attributed

factors are the important influence to cause consumers who either do not choose to buy or choose to buy its innovative products.

The attributable factor of any product may include some or all these factors. For example: Safety, durability, reasonable price, fashion, pretty design, loyalty, etc. different factors whether which attributed factor can cause the consumer feels positive emotion to prefer to choose to buy the manufacturer's innovative products. I shall recommend how to predict consumers' positive emotion to the manufacturer's products in the consumer's constructive choice process. However, the benefits to manufacturers if who can predict what attribute factors have much influence consumers to make final decision in the constructive consumer choice process. It includes as below:

● Concentrate on manufacturing the new products to predict which attribute factors are the importance existed to influence consumers' whose final decision to choose to buy the manufacturer's any kind of products in order to raise chance to increase sale numbers.

● To let consumers have more confidence to choose to buy the manufacturer's any products to use for long time.

● Avoiding to spend excess money and resources and time to concentrating on manufacturing the new product which own much of not important attribute factors to influence consumers to choose not to buy the manufacturer's products .

● Market review of constructive consumer process research limit

I feel that constructive consumer choice process can only be predicted to find whether what attributable factors can influence the consumer to choose to buy the manufacturer's product from shopping retail market only, but it can't not predicted from online shopping.

Because consumer needs to spend more time to compare different similar brands of product to find what the attributable factor(s) own(s) to the brand of product to attract who to make the final buying decision. If the consumer choose to buy the product, usually, who won't spend more time to gather the similar products' information to decide to which kind of product and who will buy the product from internet immediately. Otherwise, if the consumer choose leave home to walk to different shops to choose to buy the kind of product, who have more time to spend to different shops to compare the different brand products to make final buying decision. Hence , constructive consumer choice process will only occur at visiting shops' consumption to any individual or group consumption.

● Related Background of constructive consumer process

May constructive consumer choice process is a psychological factor to influence consumers' emotion to make final decision to buy either kind of emotion product or rational product in consumption market generally. How can product manufacturers detect consumers' emotion to judge whether their products are belonged to be more kind of emotion product or rational product during they decide to sell different kind of products or foods to consumers?

Constructive consumer choice is an important process to influence any consumers to choose to buy any products. I shall give my idea to indicate how product manufacturers can predict whether their products are belonged to be either more kind of emotional product or more kind of rational product at different suitation. It aims to reduce their negative emotion is caused to choose not buy their products from their constructive consumer choice process.

Consumer decision making trends technological change and information explosion nowadays. Generally, consumers need to compare different brands of products from their characteristics , such as quality, fashion, design style, colors, prices, functions etc. factors to decide which is the most valuable choice to buy among of these different kinds of similar products from global consumption channel, such as electronic internet shopping channel or traditional retail shopping channel of two kinds of sale methods. Due to consumers can get any kinds of products' the most updated information from internet, television , magazines etc. advertisement channel at home conveniently. Thus, it causes nowadays consumers will concern to use a variety of strategic contingent on their consumption to demand to choose to buy what is the most valuable product considerately.

After consumers spend much time to make constructive choice, who will make final decision to choose to buy which kind of product is the most valuable from their positive emotion. In general, before any consumer chooses to make decision to buy any product, whose option is in a choice it will be assumed to have a utility or subjective value feeling to the product that it depends only on the option. Finally, it is assumed that the consumer has ability of skill in a computation that enables the calculation of which option will maximize whose received value and selects accordingly.

Why are preferences constructive logic buying decision in constructive consumer choice is important? One reason individuals may construct preferences is that who lacks the cognitive resources to generate well preferences for many situations. A second important reason is that consumers often multiple goals to be given decision problem. It implies preferences constructive choice will influence any consumer to change whose emotion to prefer to buy the product among of the same kind of target products. However, the fact that a choice is contingent need not simply that the processing was constructive , that is developed on the spot. A food or soft drink can be either a rational product or emotional product. For example, a consumer may have a well established, but contingent, preference for have chocolate on a cold day and a cold soft drink on a warm day, such a preference is not constructive to influence the consumer's emotion to spend long time to compare other similar foods or drinks to make the final decision to choose to buy the chocolate or a cold soft drink among of the other similar kind of target foods or drinks in supermarket. In this situation, it seems that the chocolate and soft drink is emotional product. A major purpose , therefore is to provide a conceptual framework for understanding constructive consumer choice how to influence consumers' emotion to make final consumption decision in the rational environment only. This framework then allows to accomplish the two major goals:

(i) Reviewing consumer decision research with the framework serving as a organizing device and (ii) Using this review to gaps in my knowledge that suggest new research directions to predict consumer's individual emotion of purchasing behavior. In general, in consumer view point, consumer product motive can provide two kinds of motives . One kind is emotional product motive which persuades the consumer on the basic of whose emotion, the buyer doesn't try to reason out or typically analysis the need for purchase. Another kind is rational product motive which arises on the basic of logical analysis and proper evaluation, the buyer makes rational decision after chief evaluation of the purpose, alternatives available, cost benefit and such valid reasons.

How to predict consumer decision tasks and decision strategies? In some cases, the two options may be simply to either accept or reject an alternative. The attributes may vary in consumers' potential consequences, the product desirability to the consumer and the consumer's acceptance to make off less of one attribute for more of another. For example, a consumer may fairly certain about the values of some of the attributes. (e.g. reliability, safety factors) to the product to influence the consumer's buying decisions. For example, a consumer considers the cars to decide that safety was the most important attribute, processed only that attribute with the best value on that attribute limited effectively requires selective attention to information or a consumer might engage in attribute processing by examining the price of each of the cars. Including that car (B) was the most expensive, car (A) was the least expensive, and that (C) had a very good price. However, the consumer could process in an alternative based fashion by examining the reliability, price, safety of car (A) in order to form a overall valuation of the car. In compensatory strategy, a good value on one attribute can't make up for a poor value on another. If a consumer decide to choose the safest car, then car(D) will be chosen regardless of as high price and regardless of the high ratings for car (B) on reliability or car (E) for fashion.

● Consumer decision strategies

First step, the amount of information processed. For example, an automobile choice is as implied by most rational choice models to consider each of the available cars or it may only a consideration of a limited set of information. (e.g. repeating what one choice last time). Second step, different amount, information can be processed for each attribute or alternative (selecting processing) or same amount of information can be processed each attribute or alternative. Third step, the pattern of processing (whether by alternative (brand) or by attribute. Final step, the consumer will select to buy the product, based on whether the strategy is compensatory or non compensatory.

In addition, aspects of the environment the capture involuntary attention may set in motion and consumer behavioral responses. (e.g. in a loud environment is as a threat to cause the consumer's negative emotion to decide to buy the product). It implies quiet environment has more positive influence to consumer's individual emotion. For many consumer choice, there is little emotion involvement or need to justify. The choice goals and the extent to which different strategies accomplish these goals in different task environment. For example, proposed measured of cognitive effort and accuracy. With respect to cognitive effort, any decision strategy can be decomposed into more elementary information processes, such as reading on item of information, comparing two items of information, eliminating items of information and so on for a general decision to analyze information processing for each individual consumer when who need to choose to buy any products. For another example, a consumer can conceptualize to read the value for each attribute weight, comparing the weight just read with the largest weight found previously until the most important attributable has been found and then reading the values for the options on that attribute and comparing the until the largest value is found. It weight adding strategy could be thought as reading weights and values, multiplying the two ,moving on to the next weight and value and multiplying them, adding the product.

Consumer sometimes face emotion choice. Such choices arise when there are choice conflicts between goals that are very important to the individual. (e.g. one can't attain all goals given the set of available options and must give up something on one important goal to attain more of another important goal). Examples of such emotion consumer choices include trading off the safety of an automobile against environmental concerns (if larger vehicles fare better in crashes but worse in gas mileage) or trading health risks due to the presence of insects in one's house versus health risks from having chemicals sprayed in one's yard. Such choice can easily lead to negative emotion, since the trade-offs required represent threats to the attainment of importance or valued goals. The degree of emotion often depends on the values of the options. (e.g. the degree of conflict and which specific attributes are involved in the conflict). However, the negative emotion is caused by the consumer's choice process, it is not only caused by external environment, e.g. noise influence. Choice processes under negative emotion may therefore be affected by accuracy and effort concerns as modified by emotion minimization concerns. In particular, two general copying strategies may apply in consumer emotion situations: problem focuses copying (direct actions aimed at improving the person environment relationship to influence the consumer's emotion), and emotion focused copying (indirect actions aimed at minimizing emotion through changes in the amount or content of thought about the situation). Hence, manufacture will expect that increased negative emotion due to the choice situation will lead to more extensive processing. New products were evaluated more favorably when their attributes were moderate only when consumers had limited knowledge about the product category.

Consumers had more extensive knowledge about the category , their evaluations were influenced by associations to specific attributes based on their final choice level. Thus, knowing what the consumer's the most need of attributes of the product is very important in whose construct choice process. The affective tests consumer emotion's prediction weakness. The primary purpose of affective tests is to assess the personal response (

preference or acceptance) of current or potential customers to a product idea or a specific product characteristics. Qualitative affective tests are those (e.g. interviews and focus groups) that measure subjective response of a sample of consumers to the sample kinds of products by having those consumers talk about their feelings in an interview or small group setting. A highly trained interviewer/ moderator is required because of the high level of interaction between the interviewer/moderator and the consumers. Types of qualitative affective tests include focus groups, focus panels, mini-group and one-on-one interviews. However, qualitative affective tests will have these problems, such as with focus groups, individual answer can get lost in the group conversation. In addition, individual can reject from expressing opinions contrary to the group because of perceived peer pressure or group think. Panels which are focus group that meet repeated suffer from the same problems as focus groups. With one-on-one interview fasters might substantially temper a negative assessment of a product in order to not to appear honest answer or because they like the interviewer and don't want to hurt their feelings.

● Internet questionnaires recommendation

I recommend any individual company can send internet questionnaires to individual to detect what attribute factors can influence individual consumer's emotion to make the final consumption decision to choose to buy its innovative new products by email before their new products will be manufactured. Thus, the manufacturer can predict whether what attribute factor can be the most potential influence to individual's emotion to choose to buy whose new products generally. For example, one car manufacturer can send email questionnaires to individual consumer to invite who to fill its questionnaires in its website, these questionnaire questions can indicate as below:

(a) What attribute factor(s) can influence you to choose to buy our company's new design style sport car products?. reliability .new fashion .fast speed .brand .popular. reasonable price . durability, .safety .more functions . unique design style

(b) Which factor do you feel which is the most important to influence you to make the final buying decision to choose to buy our company's new design style sport car products ?

In general, this company's all sport cars which are rational products. It means any consumer will prefer to spend time to compare its any style of sport cars to other brands of sport cars to make final decision to choose to buy which brand of sport car. For example, if one consumer feels safety attribute factor is the most important to influence who chooses to buy any sport cars. Then, he/she will demand to attempt to drive to detect this car company's any style of sport cars to test whether which can satisfy to whose safe demand. Even, if who feel other brands' style of sport cars can satisfy whose safe demand, he/she will be possible to attempt to drive to detect other brands of similar style sports cars to compare to this brand of sport car to make final purchase decision.

Owing to there are many brands of sport cars which are provided to individual consumer to compare to choose to make final decision to buy in any country. It seems that any consumer will prefer to spend time to make logical and rational analysis to compare them and who won't be influenced by whose emotion to decide to buy any brands of sport cars in the short time easily. Thus sport cars is belonged to rational product more then emotional product.

As this reason, so I recommend this sport car company needs to prepare email questionnaires to enquire its potential individual consumer to attempt to let who to give feedback to predict whether what attribute factors can influence whose emotion to choose to buy its any kind style sport cars as well as whether what attribute factor will be the most importance to compare the other attribute factors to make final cause to influence final decision to choose to buy its any sport cars to avoid the worst attribute factor is caused. Following the car company gathers different feedback to predict whether what attribute factors are as well as what the worst factor is from these sample potential consumer's idea of its email questionnaire. Then, it can predict the result from consumers' idea to make final decision whether which are the least attractive attribute factors which will influenced any individual consumer to decide not to buy its any style of sport cars.

It aims to predict whether what are the least attractive attribute factors to cause bad emotion to the consumer to choose not to buy the kind of sport car generally. Such as, not reliable engines, old fashion , slow speed, unpopular brand, not reasonable price, not durability, not safety, less functions or not unique design style of whether which are the least attractive attribute factors. Hence, it can predict whether which attribute factors will be the attractive influence to cause its any potential consumer to choose to buy its any new innovative sport cars in order to concentrate on manufacturing any new innovative style sport cars to design which must own the most attractive attribute factors before it decides to manufacture its new style of sport cars. In conclusion, it seems that constructive consumer choice is an important process to influence any consumer to choose to buy any products. I recommend any company ought attempt to prepare questionnaires to investigate whether which the most attractive attribute factors are and which the least attractive attribute factors are influenced to each potential consumer will choose to buy or not buy to its launch innovative new products by email questionnaire channel. In general, youth people will feel ease to use online to shopping to compare to old people. I shall indicate online car brands comparison Constructive consumer choice processes

Table 1 An example of a consumer decision task
car reliability price safety speed
A worst best good very poor
B best worst worst good

C poor very good average average

D average poor best worst
E worse very good good best
Attributes are scored on seven point scales ranging from best to worst, with indicating the most desirable value for the attribute and worst indicating the least desirable value.

How to evaluate online sale method is more acceptable to sell the product.

● Explaining what situation makes the individual consumer doesn't accept to use internet technology sale channel to buy the product as well as it why internet will cause negative purchase emotion to any consumer to choose to buy any manufacturer's products .

● Abstract

The third aspect solution, I shall explain why the electronic commerce sale channel in technology acceptance model, it is possible that why it can influence the consumer's positive emotion to be changed to be negative emotion to choose not to buy the manufacturer's product . Moreover, I shall teach manufacturer whether how to judge it ought or does not ought choose this technology model to sell its products from internet channel.

● Main Problem Being Addressed

The third aspect main problem is researched why internet sale will have what bad factors to influence consumers to cause negative emotion to decide not to buy manufacturers' products from online shopping. I shall recommend how to predict their products whether which are suitable to sell from internet and how to improve their sale methods to increase consumer's positive emotion to accept to buy their products from internet. The final discussion is judged in what situation it will cause individual consumer doesn't like to enter the manufacturer's website to choose to buy the manufacturer's products.

I shall also indicate why the manufacturer will cause negative emotion to whose consumers if who chose online sale channel. I aim to teach manufacturer how to know whether whose products ought or not ought to be chose to sell from online sale channel as well as how to reduce to cause bad influence to consumers' emotion from whose websites to avoid online sale failure chance. I shall use internet surveys to gather information to detect whether what factors influence the consumer choose prefer to buy or not to prefer buy the manufacturer's products from internet as well as how manufacturers can predict consumer's emotion in the constructive consumer choice process before who choose online shopping. Hence, if the manufacturer could predict whether what weaknesses are existed to reduce whose website attraction to whose consumers' attention. It will avoid whose online sale failure. The benefits to manufacturer include who can predict what weaknesses of whose website are, then who can attempt to revise which aspects of whose website weaknesses in order to raise whose consumers' positive emotion when who uses internet to enter the sale website to find any kinds of products to buy them. If the manufacturer's website can raise attraction ability to increase many customers to see whose website. Then, whose customer numbers will be increased possibly. Online sale influence research can only apply to manufacturers who sell their products from their website sale channel.

● Related Background of internet sale channel

Nowadays, many young people like to choose to use internet to buy any manufacturer's products. Although internet is popular to accept to young to use to buy any products, but it will have chance to cause negative emotion to individual consumers from positive emotion due to they enter any manufacturer's website to find some bad points to influence their feeling to be bad. Finally, the consumers will not choose to buy the manufacturer's products due to the manufacturer does not know what the bad points are existed to whose website. Thus, I believe that internet won't be accepted to be the best sale channel to adopt to use to sell to any manufacturers' products effectively, even internet sale channel will cause some consumers negative emotion to influence who choose not to buy the manufacturer's products if the product's manufacturer chooses internet to help who to advertise whose this product to sell from internet sale channel.

Previous research has linked the experience of loneliness with materialism, suggesting that when consumers attach too great an importance to possessions, they may reduce the importance of their social relationships, leading to isolation and feelings of loneliness. Thus materialism may arises a way to cope with loneliness, which suggests that to decrease materialism, one may want to first focus on building social relationships and reducing loneliness rather than focusing first upon reduced consumption.

Hung & Mukhopadhyay (2012) examined the influence of actor versus observes perspectives on the emotional experience. "They find that "actors tend to focus move on the situation at hand and experience more emotion, such as excitement, sadness when who recall or anticipate emotional experiences. Their previous research has linked experiences of loneliness with materialism, suggesting that when consumers attach to great an importance of their social relationship, leading to isolation and feelings loneliness. This may unfortunately, lead to downward, thus it focus on building social relationship and reducing loneliness rather than focusing first upon reduced consumption." It seems social environment can influence the consumer's social emotion to choose to consume the product. The meaning of happiness that is most relevant to influence choices, such select those with a present focus will prefer products that offer calm. Thus, it seems excited consumers will choose exciting products and calm consumers will choose relaxing products. It implies that who will prefer to choose to buy the kind of product from online shopping if the consumer is a excited person to accept new technology shopping model and enjoyed to loneliness to sit down to use whose laptop to choose to buy any online products at home quiet environment. Otherwise, if consumers don't like loneliness, who will like to leave their homes to go to retail shops to buy any manufacturers' new innovate products with their friends or families and who will feel more happy and enjoyable in this non technological shopping model. Thus, it implies the enjoyable quiet environment, loneliness, technology excited consumers will choose to buy products from online sale model more. Otherwise, the enjoyable noise environment, social relationship, calm consumers will choose to buy products from traditional retail shops sale channel. Thus, consumers' emotion will be influenced to feel enjoyable or non-enjoyable to buy the product from the online shopping model or traditional visiting retail shops model .It seems that noise or quiet shopping environment will influence individual consumer's emotion to make final decision to buy the product. If the consumer enjoys to choose to buy any brands of products in the quiet environment at home lonely, the online shopping technological model will be more chance to be accepted to make final decision to this consumer habitually. Otherwise, if the consumer enjoys to choose to buy any brands of products in the noise environment, social relationship with friends, the visiting retail shops model will be more chance to be accepted to make final decision to this consumer habitually.

What is this meaning to this consumer in these two different situation? I feel that the consumer will prefer to choose to buy the kind of product from online shopping if who is a excited person, so who can accept to use internet more than visiting retail shops , due to who enjoys to loneliness to sit down to use whose laptop to choose to buy any online products at home quiet environment. Otherwise, if the consumer does not like loneliness, who will like to leave whose home to visit retail shops to choose to buy any brands of products with whose friends or families in the noise shopping center environment, due to who will feel more happy and enjoyable to buy any products in the noise and social relationship with friends or family outside environment. It means that the product manufacturer needs to understand whether whose products can be more accepted to sell to its potential consumers from either online sale model or visiting retail shops traditional sale model as well as how to design its product styles to match its potential consumers to build positive emotion whether this product is suitable to sell from online sale channel. In general, the perceived case of use can influence perceived usefulness of the product, then to influence consumer's attitude to choose to buy the product. Hence, attitude can influence the consumer's commonly. I feel that the consumer will choose to visit retail shops to test the product's functions or attempt to touch the product or see the product's actual image in the retail shops, even who needs the salespeople to teach who how to use the product when feel the product is difficult to learn to use. Specially, it is a new innovative technological product, when it will be promoted to market to sell in the first time. Due to the consumer did not know this new product existed before, who needs the salespeople talk to whom to explain how to use this new technological innovative product to listen carefully. So, who will choose to visit retail shops to decide to buy this product with whose friends or families more than online shopping. Otherwise, if the consumer feels the product is ease to use and who like loneliness, who will accept to use internet to make final decision to choose online to buy the product in the quiet home environment more than traditional visiting retail shops model. It seems the external environment and the consumer's personality can influence the consumer's emotion to make final decision to choose to buy any brand of product. For example, the consumer feels the product is ease to learn to use or difficult to learn to use. It will influence the consumer choose to buy either from online or retail shops.

● How can internet cause positive emotion to consumers?
Online shopping lacks emotion physically experienced (e.g. examined, tried on, and used), it is difficultly for shoppers with little computer expertise, there are some general uncertainties associated in homes hopping of all kinds (e.g. concerns about product return, credit card security, loss of privacy, merchant legitimacy.) Each consumer's confidence might play an important role in predicting intentions to purchase. The factors influence whose confidence which may include, such as consumer's lower perceived risk, product appearance, image size and product movement were manipulated in context of simulated appeal web sites. Both manipulations in the computer medicated environment were expected to create virtual experiences affecting mood, perceived risk and purchase intent product image size is a significant factor.
Product presentations using movement attract attention and generate good mood in on-line shoppers, even soft music listening in quiet home environment can influence consumer's emotion to cause online shopping intention. The benefits of online shopping in relation to traditional stores hopping are one of the driving forces in the adoption. Perceived usefulness has been used to explain consumer acceptance of online shopping. Perceived usefulness refers to the degree to which a person believes that using a particular system (e.g. an online shopping site) would enhance his or her job performance. Risk perception of online shopping can be

risked into two predominant types behavioral risk and environment risk. Behavioral risk arises from online retailers who have a chance to behave in an opportunistic manner by taking advantage of the government's inability to monitor all transactions adequately.

It includes product risks, psychology risks and seller performance risks. Environment risk is caused by the unpredictable nature of the purchasing medium-internet, which is beyond the control of online retailer and consumer. It includes financial risks and privacy risks. Perceived risk can be affected or moderated by a variety of factors, including consumer demographics, internet experience, product characteristics and attributes of a web site etc.

The perceived product risk varies with the age and internet experience of consumers. As consumers get older, their accumulated experience and knowledge make their stopping more targeted of certain brands and make them more confident, which can reduce product risk and the need for conducting pre-product information searches. It is possible that in comparison to make consumers female consumers perceived the likelihood and consequences of negative outcomes as a result of purchasing online to be greater and their concerns regarding these verity of the consequences of privacy loss during online shopping were stronger. The effect of perceived risk may be subject to product characteristics. The risk is generally higher for high involvement products that require the problem solving behavior and have some degree of personal importance than for low involvement products. Hence, online retailers of low involvement products may have greater success in keeping buyers than those of high involvement products, if the former can provide on appealing shopping experience. Other attributes of products do matter to perceived risk . For example, the risk was perceived lower for product for categories associated with higher expenditure levels, more satisfying characteristics and feeling and touching before purchase.

Consumer attitude is directly affected by users' belief about a system, which consist of perceived usefulness and once of use to use online to shopping in technology acceptance model to each individual consumer. In the technological acceptance model aspect view, it is possible that the consumer's perception of technology of safety and cost is important to influence who to choose to buy the product as well as self efficiency has been found to affect technology usage also through its effects on the emotional state of the user buy, for example, the manufacturer can reduce the consumer whose computer anxiety and it can increase behavioral control to its consumer more easily when its consumers enter it's product website to feel it is more safe to buy its products to compare to its online competitors' websites. Due to the characteristics of online retail context to innovative products, consumers are subjected to more influences in the virtual store where who are able to interact with an adaptive environment as a consequence on adaptive and interactive scenario is more appealing for consumers, with benefits for the decision making process. Thus, internet will influence consumers whose emotion to choose another online shopping model to any innovative products sale channel. Enjoyment can be considered the degree to which consumer perceives a certain technology as pleasant. It implies that richer technology leads to higher enjoyment for achieving a stronger influence on consumers' attitudes toward online retailers.

I shall recommend any one innovative product manufacturer ought send questionnaires by to any individual consumer by email to enquire about such as below:

(i) Do you feel this kind of innovative product is either easy or difficult more to learn to use ? It aims to predict their emotion to give feedback to let who to know whether consumers' emotion will be felt more easy or more difficult to use this product from these sample population. Then , this manufacturer can judge whether it ought to sell this kind of innovative product from either traditional retail shops or online shopping model.

(ii) Do you feel you like to buy this product in either quiet environment or noise environment more? It aims to predict their positive emotion response to judge whether who accept to buy this kinds of innovative product in the quiet environment or noise environment more to decide to make visiting retail stores channel or online sale online to sell this product.

(iii) Do you like to use internet advertisement or magazine advertisement channel to find this kind of product? It aims to predict internet online sale model or retail stores sale channel which is more acceptable to sell the manufacturer's products to attract to influence many customers to make final decision to buy its products more popular and acceptable.

(iv) Do you need salespeople to talk to you to give truly products information to assist you to buy my brand of any products? .absolutely need .absolutely not need .may be need. may not be need. It aims to judge whether the online sale is more important sale channel or not to compare with retail shops sale channel. After it gathers these statistic information from these sample potential Consumers' email questionnaires, the manufacturer can analyze whether this kind of innovate product is more acceptable from online sale model or traditional retail shopping model in its country, even global sale. Thus, it can decide either to increase to open more retail shops or decrease retail shops numbers or concentrating on selling its products from online sale channel more sale methods.

On conclusion, face reading technology and online shopping sale technology may bring positive consumption emotion to influence any customers choose to buy the kind of product when the seller can apply online webstore and face reading machine to excite consumer purchase desire . So, their products can raise price when they do not raise sale number if they apply online and face teching technology to sell their products. These technology may bring these advantges. Firstly, video camera recording technology can predict why the consumer chooses to buy the kind of product as well as face reading technology can measure whether what weights of the sugar ingredients to manufacture the weight of sweets, chocolate, soft drinks of the most good taste foods. Secondly, the manufacturer can concentrate on manufacturing whose new product which can own the most attractive attributable factor to attract which customers to choose to buy to reduce the invent lose risk. Thirdly, website sale channel must not be suitable to any manufacturers to choose to sell which products. If who can know whether their products are suitable to sell from internet or retail stores sale channel more. It can reduce the risk to loss their customers in long time. However, if you feel your product or food ought to sell from online channel. I recommend you ought need to do marketing research to evaluate whether which sale channel is the most suitable to research to sell your products or foods to persuade your clients to choose to buy. Otherwise, if your online sale channel is not suitable to sell to cause bad emotion to your clients. Thus, I believe it will reduce your client numbers due to you sell your products in the wrong sale channel.

CHAPTER SIX

Can non-manual driving public transport increase passengers number

● Reasons we need to improve public bus transport tool service quality

The ways that we need to improve public transport, e.g. bus transport service, we try our best to ask these questions: During periods of stress on the bus, like weather conditions or maintenance failure that slows the bus service system? How to improve mass transit on bus service frequency, when looking at ways to improve public bus service transport , riders want frequency? Interestingly, speed is not as much of an issue, if they are waiting downtown in the rain, or on some suburban backstreet, riders want to know that a bus will arrive soon, preferably in less than 15 minutes. Therefore, the wait becomes part of the transportation cycle. Even, if the bus is lightning fast, in the mind of the rider, the trip begins right when they arrive at the bus station, and start waiting for the bus to pick them up.

`

`What does efficient bus ticketing system mean? It is big part of how to improve bus transportation efficiency is improving transit ticketing system, because ticketing systems have to be quick and practical to allow for prompt loading and unloading of passengers. So, inefficient ticketing systems also slow down bus frequency, as drivers need to wait for everyone to tap before they can drive away to the next stop.

How to let passengers feel comfortable? Riders want comfortable buses that can seat as many people as possible. Face-to-face seating is not appealing and being knee-to-knee in a confined space creates awkward moments between strangers. However, comfort also extends beyond the buses' seating arrangements. A smooth riding, quiet bus plays a significant role in reducing the overall stress of a public transit experience. Among the consistent feedback from riders of fuel cell electric buses is a surprised delight about how quiet the buses are when in motion.

On reduce greenhouse gases environment prote3ctoin aspect, exhaust spewing buses are on ongoing concern. One of the significant factors that commuters consider when deciding to take public transit is the environment impact of their alternative transport method. And although a diesel bus packed with 40 people may be less environmentally damaging than 40 separate diesel cars, it will still have negative impacts on both local air quality and the overall climate situation , when given the choice, we've found nearly all riders prefer " zero-emission buses" to conventional diesel buses nowadays.

IN fact, we are always thinking of ways to improve public transportation by dev4eloping new clean fuel technologies. Fuel cell electric buses resolve some of the above issues for both transit bus operators, bus performance is continually being proven and improved over millions of miles of operation in environments ranging from mountain villages to desert communities to busy cities. Hence, the first step to creating better public transit networks is becoming aware of the available options. Many communities are taking measures to improve public transport by implementing innovative sustainable transport solutions that have profound impacts on the live ability of their communities.

So, I shall recommend these ways to improve public transport methods to bus service as below:

Firstly, making interchanging easy for public transport has most efficient public transport service improvement aim at linking areas that are outside a city to the city center., doing this is beneficial in two ways. It helps people who should not at the city center , but needed to pass through because the outlying areas are not connected together to keep off and hence reduce congestion at the center. Also, connecting the outlying areas provide a backup for the public transport system in case of a problem which often happen.

Secondly, minimize the number of stops/ stations, stops and stations improve the efficiency of public transport , but there should be a balance between enabling accessibility with more steps or stations and reducing the costs of operation by increasing transit need of ensure trips are covered in time. Therefore, core should be taken to ensure that stops and stations are located on streets to balance accessibility by commuters on one hand and reduces operating cost on the other hand.

Thirdly, lessen traffic congestion by deploying a number measures. Reducing traffic congestion at city streets could be done, implementing a number of strategies, such as providing lanes dedicated specially for the use of public transport, deploying strict regulations , such as queue bypasses or queue jumps. Another means of reducing traffic congestion is by providing feeds and data from public transport systems, freely to commuters to educate and help them avoid areas of traffic congestion and finally, giving priority to public and trams operating efficiency, increasing the travel time of these engineering mechanism whereby a traffic signal turns green at the light of a public transport at an intersection. All of above these improvements may be future public transport bus passengers service improvement need, if any bus companies hope to increase their bus passengers number absolutely.

● What rail passengers really want rail innovation improvement

Public transport systems, such as rail provides benefits including less traffic congestion, less pollution, safe travels, lower expenditures , less effort and better predictability in comparison to road transport. In fact, bus and train riders experience the most negative emotions in comparison with other transport modes, such as private cars , walking and cycling. Hence, technology has the potential to bring about the changes, needed to increase efficiency of rail transport, e.g. cost-effective ways to improve the quality of public transport and increase ridership may involve comfort and convenience improvement, or technology has the potential to provide more up-to-date information and customized service to train passengers and therefore improve the rail journey experience . On the overall, passenger journey , e.g. the importance of automated traveller information systems, and electronic fare payment collection systems can bring rail passengers look for this information in different interfaces from localized displays installed on platforms to smartphone applications.

Moreover, technology can also improve fare collection and management which of made manually can be prone to error, and time consuming , unified cards, smartphones can make it easier for rail passengers to obtain ticket, with the potential to increase the user satisfaction with the rail system. Because rail passengers demand not only pre-trip information for planning their travels, but also information during journeys, such as punctuality, connections and platform allocation. One extensive review indicates that accurate communication, for example, giving effective way finding information, can optimize passengers' experience with public transport.

Also, technology can facilitate the process of finding free seats on trains, which is a current demand from rail passengers and the cause of stress during the boarding process. IN fact, many rail passengers have specific preferences regarding seats and would appreciate having control of where to sit. So, navigation and way finding information can be delivered directly to passengers to inform where they could stand aiming to board less busy carriages, for example, choosing to travel on a less crowded train, or spreading themselves out on the platform before boarding in respond to crowding information, e.g. smartphones are frequently used by passengers of public transport and can make waiting times seem shorter. Furthermore specific system features designed for train passengers have the potential to improve the journey experience of the travelling public.

What ferry passengers service improvement need

● How can ferry service be improved affordable, reliable, convenient, flexible and clean will get drivers out of their cars ad onto environmentally responsible to passenger ferries?

Ferry transportation provides an environmentally friendly commuting alternative to the congested roadways in many of countries , so ferry transport service needs to meet long term air quality goals, it is critical to move beyond traditional technologies to zcro-and near zero emissions technology. Clearly putting a transit system in operation that demonstrates emission control technology and the development of zero-emissions, ferries will help achieve air quality goals to our societies, for example., new shipping rout4es are needed to increase in order to satisfy ferry passengers different rapid ferry journey short distance need, when they need to choose one kind of public transport service either bus or rail or ferry transport service among of them.

None ferry accident occurrence, ferry service needs to let passengers to feel it is the safest sea pubic transit, expanded recreational service is also needs, particularly on weekends when bridge , corridor traffic congestion is becoming an increasing problem. Ferry service needs have uniquely provided flexible, vital transportation supports in response to a natural or man-made disaster that shuts down bridges and roads, fuel –cell technology is needed , that will lead to zero-emissions ferries, e.g. on-board emissions monitoring is far less polluting than previously through, e.g. 149 passenger boats are designed to travel 25 knots or less , and 300-350 passenger vessels designed for speeds up to 30-35 knots.

This emissions standard will perform specifications and the cost of this technology is accounted for in the ferry company vessel capital budget ,e.g. vessel design capabilities to accommodate existing and new docking configurations . This maximizes fast ferry passenger loading, including bicycles, carriages and wheelchairs. Hence, future global ferry service needs have these positive influence to our societies: Need for flexibility, desire to help the environment, need for time saving, which includes the importance of reliability, sensitivity to personal travel experience, such as a need for personal space or quiet feeling ferry seat any time, insensitivity to transport cost, e.g. the ferry ticket price is cheaper than rail or bus fares sensitivity to stress.

However, ferry service is different unlike rail, bus because expanded ferry service can be launched quickly at low initial cost and with great flexibility. Unlike buses, ferries are not hindered by traffic congestion on roads and highways or in tunnels. So, ferry service can be safely expanded to bring new service to new places and add more service to existing routes more easily than bus and rail public transport both, e.g. expanded ferry transport service can operate safety and provide with a robust, flexible and effective emergency response capability if the region is hit with a natural or man-made event that disables roads, other transit, bridges , before any.

Hence, ferry companies need to decide to improve their ferry transport service, they need to answer these questions: Is the new shipping route a good transportation investment? Does the new shipping route have fatal environmental negative impact? Does it offer a transit option that can be initiated in a timely and cost-effective manner? Can it provide ferry transport service that is reliable, safe and fully accessible after the ferry recovery would be unreasonably high charge to ferry selection is decided to implement to increase?

Also, ferry safety is needed to consider because it can influence any ferry passenger choice, when the ferry is moving on the sea, when the passenger is sitting on the boat. The ferry safety issue may include: Ensuring that access to all ferry operational areas, including, machinery spaces, pilothouse and gear lockers, remain locked at all times and accessible only to authorized crew, posting night watch security guards at terminals, conducting diligent onboard inspection for unattended passenger bags, briefcases and packages after each run, before the next boat load is allowed to board, creating coded signals and response to report suspicious activity, requiring positive identification before allowing any contractors, vendors or others access to ferries, providing additional security training to crew, developing a security plan to account for potential threats, outlining preventive measures and detailing an action plan in the event of a threat or actual emergency.

Future Human Transport Need Change

How future our transport need change? What factors influence our future transport need change? In general, these factors may influence our transportation need change. They may include fuel cost, the labor market for commercial drivers, demand for frieight , customer loyalty , vehicle capacity, government regulation, geographical events, the public transport tool reputation to passegners as a merchant. However, the factors that influence the development of transport system in an area? They may include as below:

Environment at the local scale existing hydrographical and geomorphological characteristics are string, factors in transport development, particularly in terms of the tcchnical challenges (bridge, gradients,) they present to construct, other factors may include historical, technological, political and economic factors. All of these factors may influence our future transport system how develops. For raiway development influential factors, they may include: Geograohical factors, e.g. the North Indian plain with its level land, high density of population and rich agriculture presents the most favourable conditions for the development of railways in India. However, the presence of large number of rivers makes it necessary to construct bridges which involve heavy expenditure to Indian Government publich transport expenditure.

How transport has changed from past to present?

There has been a remarkable development in modern transportation. The stream engine and then the stream trains have emerged and spread at this time and in abundance until the discovery of natural gas and oil was an evolution of transportation. Thus, the sedams and vehicles began to run in oil, until present battery changes energy vehicle need, even future non-manual driving artificial intelligent driving vehicle need. These new transport technology may influence our future public transportation from gas energy to battery changed energy, even non-manual driving vehicles need to our daily transport need.

So, our future purpose of public transport need is the unique purpose to oversome space, which is shaped by a variety of human and physical constraints, such as distance, time. These both is our future main public transport need main purpose factors, short distance and reducing journey time, they influence that why we need to choose to catch any kinds of public transportation tool to replace purchase private cars to drive transport tool choice. So, future any kinds of public transport tools, they need to consider above both main factors , how to attract passengers to choose to catch themselves public transport tools choice in this competitive public transport tools market.

On the other hand, the economic importance of transportation development can be defined as improving the welfare of a society, through appropriate social, political and economic conditions , such as US Government spent too much money to assist MTR (MAss transport railway firm) to develop underground thrain transport. Its aim to let many passegner can reduce journey time and reduce distance between destinations, it also hopes US citizen passengers can pay cheap transport fare to buy ticket to catch underground transport train for many families their transport expenditure in social transport welfare view.

However, US Government neds to solve those challenges, before it implements to develop rapid underground railway , e.g. lack of knowledge of geographical fwatures, lack of manpower necessary to operate the rapid underground railway construction work, lack of construction materials within the US itself. For Brazil rail network transportation development example, the factors influence the use of rail network for transportion is highly restricted in Brazil. Thus, the development of roadways and waterways is the main modes of transportation that caould be used in Brazil given its topography and drainage benefit to society . So, brazil can develop rail network for transportation development in success.

So, transportation system is important in the development of any nation, because transportation plays important role in rapid economic growth of a nation. Thrapsortation increases the quality and variety of consumer goods, thereby stimulating the demand and development of trade and economy of the nation. Moreover, transport provides various employment opportunities and boosts up the economy of the country.

Also, any transport tools need to improve themselves transport service in order to attract passengers to choose their public transport service more easily. They may attempt to sign up for an autonomous vehicle pilot program, free phone enquiey concerns whether the passegner can catch which bus bumber to go to the destination, hou much bus fare, how long journey time, when the bus will arrive teh bus stops or leave the bus stop etc. bus service questions, before any one passenger prepares to choose to catch bus (free bus go phone call enquiry), free download a public transport tool transit app. even water taxi tranport tool innovation can replace ferry public transport tool, it can let passengers have more fun an enjoyable catching feeling. So, water taxi tranport tool is one kind of future new transport tool change to replace ferry , it can influence ferry passengers to choose water taxi public transport tool to replace ferry. Although, its fare may be more expsnse to compare ferry, but it can reduce jounrey time and distance between both water stations, when ferry can not arrive the other destinations, but water taxi can arrive any one water station destination. It can bring convenient to future any one ferry passengers. So, water taxi may be developed to some countries, e.g. New Zealand , Auckland city, US , Washington and New York cities they had developed water taxi public transport tools to let ferry passengers have one kind new water public transport choice.

However, instead of new transport innovation improvement to water transport service public transport with input from the public on bus transport service aspect, bus frequency improvement, it means when booking at ways to improve, bus frequency from long times to less times, efficient bus ticketing system, a big part of how to improve tranportation efficiency is improving transit ticketing system.

In fact, my future transport system may still include these five types, modes of transport are: railway, roadways, airways, waterways and piplelines. Also, among different includes of transport, railways are the different modes of transport, railways are the cheapest. Trains cover the distance in less time and comparatively, the fare is also less to other modes of transporation. Therefore, railways is the cheapest mode of transportation to compare ferry, water taxi , sea transport, bus, taxi, road system.

On conclusion, transport price is not the main factor to attract passegners to choose to catch. The importance to have a good public transport system in place. It may be one main factor to help the kind of public transport tool to attract passengers to choose to catch, because a good transport links can widen people's job search area and help them find employment. It can also reduce commuting times and reduce the cost of living, and high skilled workers are more likely to travel across longer distances to work, especially if they are following good job opportunities. So, future any one kind of public transportation tool service provider ought consider how to satisfy working people working time need to shorten journey time to any working places or student learning time need to shorten jounrey times to any schools as well as let they feel comfortable to sit on comfortable chairs or provide free internet service to themselves mobiles , laptops, when they are sitting down or standing up in the kind of public transport . It is the important factor to influence any kind of public transport service in success.

Future Non-Manual driving vehicle How
Influences Public Transport Tool Passenger Need

Nowadays, artifical intelligent (non-manual) driving vehicles are invented, it may be accepted to any countries families to feel comfortable to drive on roads, because any people choose to buy any kinds cars, when any people choose to buy kinds of non-manual (artificial intelligent) vehicles, they do not need to use their hands to drive cars, because artificial intelligent (robotic auto control wheels, it means that robots can help human (drivers) to control wheel to drive to avoid any cars crash occurrence on the roads more easily.

If one day, non-manual driving robotic control whoole vehicles are invented in successful, whether it will persuade many different conuntries families choose to buy non-manual (robotic auto control wheel) vehicles, then it will cause bus, tram, train, underground train, road transport need will be influenced to reduce or even if non-manula boats are invented, whether it will cause ferry sea transport needs will b influenced to reduce. Hence, future non-manual driving vehicles or bats invention whether they will influence public transport tool of road and sea transport passengers number reduces. It is one interesting question. I shall attempt to discuss as below:

In fact, non-manual vehicles are very attraction, to excite any person chooses to buy to drive, because people do not need often touch wheels and touch foots button to control cars to move often forever, when robotic can be invented to help human to control car wheel and foot button, any person only needs to sit on his/her car, then the car can move rapidly, because any drivers is lazy, he/she hopes machine can help her/him to drive car on the road safely. So, he/she can read book or listen music or eatch mobile movie to enjoy his/her entertainment when he/she is sitting on his/her car.He/she will feel more comfortable and enjoyable when robotic can help him/her to drive car. So, robotic (non -manual driving vehicle) can encourage people to choose to buy cars because any drivers won't need to drive cars, robotic can help drivers them to drive on the road easily, when global any one family can own one robotic auto control (non-manual driving) car at least, it may influence these owning non-manula diriving vehicle owners do not feel need to pay any fares to buy road public transport tools of bus ticket, train ticket, underground train ticket , tram ticket to go to anywhere. So, it seems that robotic (non-manual driving) vehicles may influence future any road transport passengers number reduces , because traditional catching any kinds of road public transport tool passengers will be influenced to choose to sit themselves auto (non-manual) driving cars to go to offices to work, parents do not need to follow their sone/daughters to sit on themselves non-manual auto driving cars to go to schools, because their sons/daughters can sit on themselves non-manual driving cars to go to schools more easily. In holidays, they can sit on themselves non-manual driving cars to go to cinemas, music halls, breachs, theaters, shopping centers, gardens different entertainment places to enjoy their any leisure safely because robotic can help them to drive their cars on roads safely.

So, it means that robotic auto control driving cars can influence global every family to feel that they do not need to catch any kinds of public transport tools, e.g. bus, train, tram, taxi underground train to go to anywhere because robotic auto driving cars can help any one, he/she does not know how to drive car to go to anywhere safely. So, future any one won't need to learn driving car skill, when he/she likes to buy one auto driving car. So, in passenger public transport need view, non-manual driving cars will influence them to feel any kinds of road public transport tools can help them to go to anywhere conveniently, because themselves non-manual driving vehicles can help them to drive cars to go to anywhere conveniently. They only need to tell robotic that where they want to go, when they sit on their non-manual driving cars, then robotic knows whether where destination, they want to go, their cars will auto move on the road immediately. It is one exciting and enjoyable ourney when the driver does not need to drive his/her car on the road. So, it seems that robotic (non-manual driving) vehicles invention may bring negative influence to any kinds of public transport tools service needs to passengers , when passengers had owned one non-manual driving car at least.

Why and how non-manual driving car owners need

raise public transport quality on travel time and fare

● How non human driving behavior can be influence by non-manual driving cars

In fact, impact of automated vehicless on travel mode preference, it can bring both trip purposes and distances aim raising need to any kinds of public transport service passegners. Because of technology penetration in the transportation system, the automated vehicle is set to be a future mode of transport, it may bring negative impact to future any kinds of public transport passengers needs, in special on the potential impact of these non-manual driving automated vehicles on travel behaior negative impact to public transport passenger behavior. Automated vehicles will influence future public transportation passengers feel it can bring more short time travel distances and short trip purposes more benefit than any kinds of public transport choices, e.g. bus, taxi, ferry, train, tram, underground tram etc. road and sea public transport tools, e.g. ferry, water taxi. It means that when future any passenger feels above these any one kind of public transport tool needs to spend longer travel time on journey distance and trip to compare future automated vehicles, then they will choose to sit on automated vehicles in preference, due to automated vehicles can help global any one person needs to go to anywhere rapidly.

So, automated vehicles may replace general traditional public transport tools in possible, when they are popular accepted in societies. On the other, instead of shortening journey travel distance time, (travel time) aspect, public transport fare, travel cost will be another influential factor to influence future public transport tool passengers to choose automated vehicles to replace to catch any kinds of public transport tools.

In fact, conventional cars and public transport s are perceivd as being the least attractive alternative in relation to in-vehicle travel time on short and long distance communting trips. So , future automated vehicle drivers (non -human driving) behaviors will be likely changed to prefer this mode for long distance leisure trips rather than short distance commuting trips by automated vehicles.

In fact, advanced technologies have revolutionized many aspects of human life, include the automated vehicle transport system. Also, transport system is one of the essential development aspect to particular , such as non-manual driving automation , vehicle aims to make trips safer, faster , more efficient, automated vehicles passengers and drivers can feel enjoyable to do themselves leisure behavior , e.g. read books, listen, music, listen mobile, watch laptop movies when any one does not need to consider whether their cars are safe to be driven , even any one needs to drive the automated car, because robotic can help them to control how to automatic drive this car on the road safely.

Robotic will bring confidence to let them feel that themselves cars are moving safely on the roads . In recent years, the concept of automated driving has been introduced as on outstanding platform for the next generation of driving systems that is expected to improve safety, traffic flows efficiency, reducing traffic jams occurrence chance, avoiding traffic accidents occurrence chance, e.g. avoid to crash any one person when he/ she is walking across road or crach any car is moving on the road easily, capacity, accessibility , and reducing congestion through the application of some technologies , such as vehicle to vehicle and vehicle to infrastructure communication.

So, future automated vechicles can have good driving facility systems to be installed in their cars, in order to raise safety, rapid driving speed level to let any one to feel , when they are sitting in their automated cars, e.g. using cameras, sensors, global positioning system adaptive cruise control, light detection and ranging, and advanced driver assistance system, automated vehicles can steer the vehicle and drive it automatically when passengers delegate control to a computer. Absolutely, ny replacing the driver role with an automated driving system , future one automated vehicle is able to totally free up passengers under automation levels.

So, unless future any kinds of public transport tools may apply automated robotic automated driven system replace the bus driver, taxi driver, train driver, tram driver, underground train driver to raise automated driving system service improvement level to let any one passengers to feel. Otherwise, when automated vehicles are popular to be accepted to buy in any one country in global. Then, global public tansport tool passegners number may be influenced to reduce when global any one family owns at least one automated vehicle at themselves homes .

In other words, automated vehicles can bring thes benefits to let global any one household family feels, future automated vehicles users , they can mostly behave like passengers inside the vehicle, which implies that they will be able to multitask and productive by allocating the travel time to do other activities, e.g. reading, eating, working, drinking, watching movies, listening musics, even sleeping. So, automated vechicles will motivate humans to change non-humanly driven behaviors from conventional humanly driven behavior. This non-humanly driven behavior may be one main factor to influence or encourage future any one kind of public transport passenger won't choose to pay fare to buy ticket to catch any one kind of public transport tool again, because non-manual driven behavior may hel many lazy people do not need to consdierate how to learn to drive cars skills to prepare pass any road test in order to earn the driving licnece to permit to drive cars forever. When automated vehiclesa re popular to be accepted to replace manual-driven cars in societies.

Hence, automated vehicles could potentially change the traditional human driven vehicle market to cause their manual driven cars sale buyers number reduces, when the automated vehicle buyers number increases, also they can chance globa public transport passengers behaviors to reduce to pay fares to catch any kinds of public transport tools when automated vechicles users may sit on themselves automated vehicles to go to anywhere in short time rapidly and safely in any countries.

On conclusion, future global public transport service competition is serious, because instead of global passengers had began to compare whether which kinds of public transport fares are cheaper, more safe, shortening journey time between leaving place and destination, more comfortable feeling, e.g. clean and comfortable chairs , mre free internet service facilities in order to make any one kind of catching public transport tool choice in preference. On the other hand, future automated vehicles number will increase when traditional manual driven car users begin to believe that automated vehicles can bring more safe , more comfortable, more fee-time using, more leisure satisfactory feeling, more than traditional manual driving cars. Then, when global any one household family had made choice to buy at least one automated vehice to replace themselves car(s) at home. When, they are habit to sit in themselves automated vehicles to go to anywhere, however, short or long trip . Consequently, global any one household family won't feel any kinds of public transport tools may bring personal economic saving cost, comfortable, enjoyable, free-time using benefit to compare themselves automated vehicles . It will cause global public transport tools passengers number will reduce , when many different kinds of home automatic vehicles are purchased to replace manual driving cars by global household automated vehicle users. So, in passegner transport tool choice psychological view, automatic vehicles will be possible to replace future public transport service tools. So, any public transport service providers can not neglect how to desing and improve their facilities , charge reasonable transport fare, provide more comfortable, and enjoyable sitting feeling , even applying automatic driving system to replace human drivers in order to attract passegners ' catching need choice more easily.

Reference

Reference

Howlwy, M (2002). The role of consultancies in New Product Development. Journal of product & brand management, 11(7), 477-58.

Hartwell, R.M. (1983). The origins of capitalism. A Methodological Eassy. in Pejovich (1983).

Needham, J. (1963), Poverties and Triumphs of the Chinese scientific tradition, in Crombie (1963).

Rogers,E.M. (2003) Diffusion of innovation, 5th edition, New York: Simon & Schuster.

The Times (2002) Mobile phone sales fall, The Times , 12 mar 25.

Wong, V. (2002). Antecedents of international New product pollout timeliness. Internaional marketing review, 19 (2/3), 120-32

Ambady, N. and Rosenthal, R.(1992)' Thin Silces Of Behavior As Predictors Of Interpersonal Consequences: A meta- analysis, psychological Bulletin, 2: 256-74

Arnade, E. (2014) Journal Of Consumer Research, Make a face: Implict and explict measurement of facial expression by orange juices using face reading technology. Food quality and preference, vol.32, p.161-172. Retrieved: http://hdl.handle.net/10919/54538.

Carrere, S. and Gottman, J. (1999) ' predicting divorce amongnewlyweds from the first three minutes of a marital conflice discussion', family processes 38:293-301.

Hung & Mukhopadhyay.(June 2012), Emotion And Consumer Behavior, , vol. 40 no.5 (June 2012), 39-50.

Meservy, T.O. jnsen, M.L. Kruse, W.J., Burgoo, J.K. and Nunamaker Jr., J.F. (2008) ' Automatic extraction of deceptive behavioral cues from video', in H.Chen, E. Reid, J. Sinai, A. Silke and B. Ganor (eds) Terrorism Informatics (pp. 495-516), New York: Springer.

Miller, K. (2012), Consumer behavior, Washington, USA. Retrieved: http://www.amazon.com

Palmer (2012), Consumer behavior and credit card payment, Journal of management market resarch.

Webb et. al (2000), The impact of perceived corporate social responsibility on consumer behavior, Journal of business research 59(1): pp. 46-53 Jan.

2006.

www.ingramcontent.com/pod-product-compliance
Lightning Source LLC
Chambersburg PA
CBHW071447130726
47997CB00006B/2262